Conan Doyle's War

ARTHUR CONAN DOYLE

AMBERLEY

First published 2014

Amberley Publishing
The Hill, Stroud
Gloucestershire, GL5 4EP

www.amberley-books.com

British Library Cataloguing in Publication Data.
A catalogue record for this book is available from the British Library.

ISBN 978 1 4456 4201 7 (paperback)
ISBN 978 1 4456 4209 3 (ebook)

Typeset in 11pt on 14pt Minion.
Typesetting and Origination by Amberley Publishing.
Printed in the UK.

Contents

Preface

IT is continually stated that it is impossible to bring out at the present time any accurate history of the war. No doubt this is true so far as some points of the larger strategy are concerned, for the motives at the back of them have not yet been cleared up. It is true also as regards many incidents which have exercised the minds of statesmen and of many possibilities which have worried the soldiers. But so far as the actual early events of our own campaign upon the Continent are concerned there is no reason why the approximate truth should not now be collected and set forth. I believe that the narrative in this volume will in the main stand the test of time, and that the changes of the future will consist of additions rather than of alterations or subtractions.

The present volume deals only with the events of 1914 in the British fighting-line in France and Belgium. A second volume dealing with 1915 will be published within a few months. It is intended that a third volume, covering the current year, shall carry on this contemporary narrative of a tremendous episode.

From the first days of the war I have devoted much of my time to the accumulation of evidence from first-hand sources as to the various happenings of these great days. I have built up my narrative from letters, diaries, and interviews from the hand or lips of men who have been soldiers in our armies, the deeds of which it was my ambition to understand and to chronicle. In many cases I have been privileged to submit my descriptions of the principal incidents to prominent actors in them, and to receive their corrections or endorsement. I can say with certainty, therefore, that a great deal of this work is not only accurate, but that it is very precisely correct in its detail. The necessary restrictions which forbade the mention of numbered units have now been removed, a change made possible by the very general rearrangements which have recently taken place. I am able, therefore, to deal freely with my material. As that material is not always equally full, it may have occasionally led to a want of proportion, where the brigade occupies a line and the battalion a paragraph. In extenuation of such faults, and of the omissions which are unavoidable, I can only plead the difficulty of the task and throw myself upon the reader's good nature. Some compensation for such shortcoming may be found in the fact that a narrative written at the time reflects the warm emotions which these events aroused amongst us more clearly than the more measured story of the future historian can do.

It may seem that the political chapters are somewhat long for a military work, but the reader will find that in subsequent volumes there are no further politics, so that this survey of the European conditions of 1914 is a lead up to the whole long narrative of the actual contest.

I would thank my innumerable correspondents (whom I may not name) for their very great help. I would also admit the profit which I have derived from reading Coleman's *Mons To Ypres*, and especially Lord Ernest Hamilton's *The First Seven Divisions*. These books added some new facts, and enabled me to check many old ones. Finally, I desire to thank my friend Mr. P.L. Forbes for his kind and intelligent assistance in arranging my material.

ARTHUR CONAN DOYLE,
WINDLESHAM, CROWBOROUGH,
October 1916.

The Opening of the War

THERE can be no doubt that if Germany had confined her operations to an attack upon France without any infraction of Belgian neutrality, the situation in Great Britain would have been extraordinarily difficult. The Government was the most democratic that has ever been known in our political history, and it owed its power to an electorate, many of whom were passionate advocates for peace at almost any conceivable price. The preparations for naval war, necessitated by the ever-growing German power, had been accompanied and occasionally retarded by a constant murmur of remonstrance which swelled periodically into a menacing expostulation. McKenna and Churchill found their only opponents in the members of their own party, who persistently refused to look obvious facts in the face, and impatiently swept aside the figures of the German armaments while they indulged in vague and amiable aspirations towards international friendship. This large and energetic party would certainly have most strenuously resisted British interference in a Continental war. The statesmen who foresaw that the conquest of France would surely lead to the conquest of Britain might have carried the country with them, but none the less they would have gone to war with such an incubus upon them as the traitorous Charles James Fox and his party had been in the days of Napoleon. A disunited British against a united German Empire would have been a grievous disadvantage, be our allies who they might, for, as Shakespeare sang, "If England to herself be true," it is then only that she is formidable.

This great misfortune, however, was obviated by the policy of Germany. The most peace-loving Briton could not face the national dishonour which would have been eternally branded upon him had his country without an effort allowed its guarantee to be treated as waste paper by a great military nation. The whole people were welded into one, and save for a few freakish individuals who obeyed their own perversity of mind or passion for notoriety, the country was united as it has never been in history. A just war seemed to touch the land with some magic wand, which healed all dissensions and merged into one national whole those vivid controversies which are, in fact, a sign rather of intense vitality than of degeneration. In a moment the faddist forgot his fad, the capitalist his grievance against taxation, the Labour man his feud against Capital, the Tory his hatred of the Government, even the woman her craving for the vote. A political millennium seemed to have dawned. Best and most important of all was the evident sign that the work done of late years to win the friendship of Ireland had not been in vain. If the mere promise of domestic institutions has ranged all responsible Irishmen upon one side on the day of battle, what may we not hope for ourselves and for the Empire when they have been fully established and Time has alleviated the last lingering memories of an evil past? It is true that at a later period of the war this fair prospect was somewhat overcast by an insane rebellion, in which the wrongs of Ireland, once formidable and now trivial, were allowed by a colossal selfishness to outweigh the martyrdom of Belgium and the mutilation of France. Still the fact remains (and it must sustain us in our future efforts for conciliation) that never before have we had the representative nationalists of Ireland as our allies in a great struggle.

The leaders of the Unionist party, Lord Lansdowne and Mr Bonar Law, had already, on August 2, signified to the Government that they considered Britain to be honour-bound to France, and would support without hesitation every practical step to give effect to the alliance. Fortified by this assurance, the Government could go strongly forward. But after the Belgian infraction, its position was that of the executive of a united nation. Sir Edward Grey's analysis in Parliament of the causes which had brought us to war convinced the reason and claimed the sympathy of every political party, and even the most fervent advocates of peace found themselves silenced in the presence of the huge German aggression which could never admit of a peace founded upon mutual respect and equality, but only of that which comes from ascendancy on the one side and helplessness upon the other.

Should Britain ever be led into an unjust war, she will soon learn it from the fearless voices of her children. The independent young nations which are rising under the red-crossed flag will not be dragged, in the train of the Mother-Country, into any enterprise of which their conscience does not approve. But now their assent was whole-hearted. They were vehement in their approval of the firm stand made for the pledged word of the nation. From every quarter of the world deep answered deep in its assurance that the sword should not be sheathed until the wrong was righted and avenged.

Strong, earnest Canada sent her 30,000 men, with her promise of more. Fiery Australia and New Zealand prepared as many, Maori vying with white man in his loyalty to the flag. South Africa, under the splendid leadership of Botha, began to arm, to speak with the foe in her own gates. India poured forth money and men with a lavish generosity which can never be forgotten in this country. The throb of loyalty to the old land passed through every smallest Dependency, and then beyond the frontier to those further lands which had known us as a just and kindly neighbour. Newfoundland voted a contingent. Ceylon sent of her best. Little Fiji mustered her company of fighting men, and even the mountains of Nepaul and the inaccessible plateaux of Thibet were desirous of swelling that great host, gathered from many races, but all under the one banner which meant to each a just and liberal rule.

On the very eve of the outbreak of hostilities one man was added to the home establishment whose presence was worth many army corps. This was Lord Kitchener, whose boat was actually lying with steam up to bear him away upon a foreign mission, when, at the last instant, either the universal public demand or the good sense of the Government recalled him to take supreme charge of the war. It was a strange and a novel situation that a soldier who was no party politician should assume the role of War Minister in a political Cabinet, but the times called for decided measures, and this was among them. From that day onwards until the dark hour which called him from his uncompleted task the passer-by who looked up at the massive front of the War Office was gladdened by the thought that somewhere in the heart of it those stern, immutable eyes were looking out at Britain's enemies, and that clear, calculating brain was working for their downfall. Slow, safe, methodical, remorseless, carefully preparing the means at every stage that led him to the distant but preordained end, he had shown, both in the Soudan and South Africa, that the race of great British generals was not yet extinct. He knew and trusted his instrument even as it knew and trusted him.

That instrument was an army which was remarkably well prepared for its work. It cannot be said that the Boer War had increased the prestige of the British forces, though only those who have studied the subject can realise how difficult was the task with which they were then faced, or how considerable an achievement it was to bring it to a success. But the campaign had left behind it a valuable legacy, all the richer because so great a proportion of the land forces had been drawn into the struggle. In 1914 a large proportion of senior officers and a considerable number of non-commissioned officers and reservists had passed through that ordeal, and learned by experience what can be done, and, even more important, what cannot be done, in face of modern rifles in skilful hands.

The lesson had been well pressed home after the war, and every general, from Lord Roberts downwards, had laid emphasis upon the importance of cover and of accuracy of fire. Apart from the sound technical training of the soldiers, the administration of the Army had, after an experimental period, fallen into the hands of Lord Haldane, who has left his mark more deeply than any one since Cardwell upon the formation of the land forces. A debt of gratitude is owing to him for his clear thought and his masterful dispositions. Had he been a prophet as well as organiser, he would no doubt have held his hand before he made the smallest decrease of our regular forces; but, on the other hand, by turning our haphazard, amateurish volunteers into the workman-like Territorials, in forming the invaluable

Officers' Training Corps which tapped our public schools for something better than athletic talent, and in rigidly defining our expeditionary corps and providing the special reserves for its reinforcements, he did work for which he can never adequately be thanked. The weapon which he had fashioned was now thrust into the strong right hand of the new Minister of War.

Want of space and accurate material make it impossible to do justice here to the deeds of our Allies, but an attempt must be made to indicate briefly the main phases of the struggle abroad, since its course reacted continually upon the British operations. It may be shortly stated, then, that so far as the western theatre of war was concerned, hostilities commenced by two movements, one an attack by the French upon the occupants of those lost provinces for which they had mourned during forty-four years, and the other the advance of the Germans over the Belgian frontier.

The former was a matter of no great importance. It took two distinct lines, the one from the Belfort region into Alsace, and the other from Nancy as a centre into Lorraine. The Alsatian venture gained some ground which was never wholly lost, and was adorned by one small victory near Mülhausen before it was checked by the German defence. The Lorraine advance had also some initial success, but was finally thrown back on August 20 in a severe action in which the French were defeated. Luneville, across the French frontier, was occupied by the Germans, but they made no headway, and their subsequent attempts upon Nancy were repulsed by the army of General Castelnau. General Pau, a fiery, one-armed septuagenarian, was the French leader in the Alsatian invasion, but it was soon realised by General Joffre that he and the bulk of his men would be more useful at the vital point upon the northern frontier, to which early in September they were transferred.

The main drama, however, quickly unfolded upon the Belgian frontier. Speed and secrecy were vital to the German plans. On July 31, before any declaration of war, and while the German representative at Brussels was perjuring his soul in his country's service by representing that no infringement was possible, three German army corps, the seventh, ninth, and tenth, fully mobilised and highly equipped, were moving up from their quarters so as to be ready for a treacherous pounce upon their little neighbour whom they were pledged to defend. Von Emmich was in command. On the night of Saturday, August 1, the vanguard of the German armies, using motor traffic followed by trains, burst through the neutral Duchy of Luxemburg, and on August 3 they were over the Belgian line at Verviers. The long-meditated crime had been done, and, with loud appeals to God, Germany began her fatal campaign by deliberate perjury and arrogant disdain for treaties. God accepted the appeal, and swiftly showed how the weakest State with absolute right upon its side may bring to naught all the crafty plottings of the strong. For time was the essence of the situation. For this the innumerable motors, for this the light equipment and the lack of transport. It was on, on, at the top speed, that there be no hindrance in the path of the great hosts that soon would be closing up behind. But time was life and death for the French also, with their slower mobilisation, their backward preparation, and their expectations from Great Britain. Time was the precious gift which little Belgium gave to the Allies. She gave them days and days, and every day worth an army corps. The Germans had crossed the Meuse, had taken Visé, and then had rushed at Liège, even as the Japanese had rushed at Port Arthur. With all their military lore, they had not learned the lesson which was taught so clearly in 1904 – that a fortress is taken by skill and not by violence alone.

Leman, a great soldier, defended the forts built by Brialmont. Both defender and designer were justified of their work. On August 5 the seventh German Corps attempted to rush the gaps between the forts. These gaps were three miles wide, but were filled with entrenched infantry. The attack was boldly pressed home, but it completely failed. The German loss was considerable. Two other corps were called up, and again on August 7 the attack was renewed, but with no better result. The defenders fought as befitted the descendants of those Belgae whom Caesar pronounced to be the bravest of the Gauls, or of that Walloon Guard which had so great a mediaeval reputation. There were 25,000 in the town and 120,000 outside, but they were still outside at the end of the assault.

Liège, however, had one fatal weakness. Its garrison was far too small to cover the ground. With twelve forts three miles apart it is clear that there were intervals of, roughly, thirty-six miles to be covered, and that a garrison of 25,000 men, when you had deducted the gunners for the forts, hardly left the thinnest skirmish line to cover the ground. So long as the Germans attacked upon a narrow front they could be held. The instant that they spread out there were bound to be places where they could march almost unopposed into the town. This was what occurred. The town was penetrated, but the forts were intact. General Leman, meanwhile, seeing that the town itself was indefensible, had sent the garrison out before the place was surrounded. Many a Belgian soldier fought upon the Yser and helped to turn the tide of that crowning conflict who would have been a prisoner in Germany had it not been for the foresight and the decision of General Leman.

The Germans were in the town upon the 8th, but the forts still held out and the general advance was grievously impeded. Day followed day, and each beyond price to the Allies. Germany had secretly prepared certain monstrous engines of war – one more proof, if proof were needed, that the conflict had been prearranged and deliberately provoked. These were huge cannon of a dimension never before cast – 42 centimetres in bore. More mobile and hardly less effective were some smaller howitzers of 28-centimetre calibre said to have come from the Austrian foundries at Skoda. Brialmont, when he erected his concrete and iron cupolas, had not foreseen the Thor's hammer which would be brought to crush them. One after another they were smashed like eggs. The heroic Leman was dug out from under the debris of the last fort and lived to tell of his miraculous escape. Liège was at last in the hands of the invaders. But already the second week of August was at an end – the British were crowding into France, the French line was thickening along the frontier – all was well with the Allies. Little David had left a grievous mark upon Goliath.

The German mobilisation was now complete, and the whole vast host, over a million strong, poured over the frontier. Never was seen such an army, so accurate and scientific in its general conception, so perfect in its detail. Nothing had been omitted from its equipment which the most thorough of nations, after years of careful preparation, could devise. In motor transport, artillery, machine guns, and all the technique of war they were unrivalled. The men themselves were of high heart and grand physique. By some twisted process of reasoning founded upon false information they had been persuaded that this most aggressive and unnecessary of wars was in some way a war of self-defence, for it was put to them that unless they attacked their neighbours now, their neighbours would certainly some day or other attack them. Hence, they were filled with patriotic ardour and a real conviction that they were protecting their beloved Fatherland. One could not but admire their self-sacrificing devotion, though in the dry light of truth and reason they stood forth as the tools of tyranny, the champions of barbarous political reaction and the bullies of Europe. It was an ominous fact that the troops were provided in advance with incendiary discs for the firing of dwellings, which shows that the orgy of destruction and cruelty which disgraced the name of the German Army in Belgium and in the north of France was prearranged by some central force, whose responsibility in this matter can only be described as terrific. They brought the world of Christ back to the days of Odin, and changed a civilised campaign to an inroad of pagan Danes. This wicked central force could only be the Chief Staff of the Army, and in the last instance the Emperor himself. Had Napoleon conducted his campaigns with as little scruple as William II., it can safely be said that Europe as we know it would hardly exist to-day, and the monuments of antiquity and learning would have been wiped from the face of the globe. It is an evil precedent to be expunged from the records for ever – all the more evil because it was practised by a strong nation on a weak one and on a defenceless people by one which had pledged themselves to defend them. That it was in no wise caused by any actions upon the part of the Belgians is clearly proved by the fact that similar atrocities were committed by the German Army the moment they crossed the frontiers both of France and of Poland.

The Allies had more than they expected from Liège. They had less from Namur. The grey-green tide of German invasion had swept the Belgian resistance before it, had flooded into Brussels, and had been dammed for only a very few days by the great frontier fortress, though it was counted as stronger than Liège. The fact was that the Germans had now learned their lesson. Never again would they imagine that the *Furor Teutonicus* alone could carry a walled city. The fatal guns were brought up again and the forts were crushed with mechanical precision, while the defenders between the forts, after enduring for ten hours a severe shelling, withdrew from their trenches. On August 22 the fortress surrendered, some of General Michel's garrison being taken, but a considerable proportion effecting its retreat with the French Army which had come up to support the town. By the third week of August the remains of the Belgian forces had taken refuge in Antwerp, and the Germans, having made a wide sweep with their right wing through Brussels, were descending in a two-hundred-mile line upon Northern France.

The French plans had in truth been somewhat disarranged by the Belgian resistance, for the chivalrous spirit of the nation would not permit that their gallant friends be unsupported. Fresh dispositions had been made, but the sudden fall of Namur brought them to naught. Before that untoward event the French had won a small but indubitable victory at Dinant, and had advanced their line from Namur on the right to Charleroi on the left. With the fall of Namur their long wall had lost its corner bastion, and they were at once vigorously attacked by all the German armies, who forced the Sambre on August 22, carried Charleroi, and pushed the French back with considerable loss of guns and prisoners along the whole line. There was defeat, but there was nothing in the nature of a rout or of an envelopment. The line fell back fighting tooth and nail, but none the less Northern France was thrown open to the invaders. In this general movement the British forces were involved, and we now turn to a more particular and detailed account of what befell them during these most momentous days.

The Battle of Mons

THE bulk of the British Expeditionary Force passed over to France under cover of darkness on the nights of August 12 and 13, 1914. The movement, which included four infantry divisions and a cavalry division, necessitated the transportation of approximately 90,000 men, 15,000 horses, and 400 guns. It is doubtful if so large a host has ever been moved by water in so short a time in all the annals of military history. There was drama in the secrecy and celerity of the affair. Two canvas walls converging into a funnel screened the approaches to Southampton Dock. All beyond was darkness and mystery. Down this fatal funnel passed the flower of the youth of Britain, and their folk saw them no more. They had embarked upon the great adventure of the German War. The crowds in the streets saw the last serried files vanish into the darkness of the docks, heard the measured tramp upon the stone quays dying farther away in the silence of the night, until at last all was still and the great steamers were pushing out into the darkness.

No finer force for technical efficiency, and no body of men more hothearted in their keen desire to serve their country, have ever left the shores of Britain. It is a conservative estimate to say that within four months a half of their number were either dead or in the hospitals. They were destined for great glory, and for that great loss which is the measure of their glory.

Belated pedestrians upon the beach of the southern towns have recorded their impression of that amazing spectacle. In the clear summer night the wall of transports seemed to stretch from horizon to horizon. Guardian warships flanked the mighty column, while swift shadows shooting across the surface of the sea showed where the torpedo-boats and scouts were nosing and ferreting for any possible enemy. But far away, hundreds of miles to the north, lay the real protection of the flotilla, where the smooth waters of the Heligoland Bight were broken by the sudden rise and dip of the blockading periscopes.

Such, was the Army which first set forth to measure itself against the soldiers of Germany. Prussian bravery, capacity, and organising power had a high reputation among us, and yet we awaited the result with every confidence, if the odds of numbers were not overwhelming. It was generally known that during the period since the last war the training of the troops had greatly progressed, and many of the men, with nearly all the senior officers, had had experience in the arduous campaign of South Africa. They could also claim those advantages which volunteer troops may hope to have over conscripts. At the same time there was no tendency to underrate the earnest patriotism of our opponents, and we were well aware that even the numerous Socialists who filled their ranks were persuaded, incredible as it may seem, that the Fatherland was really attacked, and were whole-hearted in its defence.

The crossing was safely effected. It has always been the traditional privilege of the British public to grumble at their public servants and to speak of "muddling through" to victory. No doubt the criticism has often been deserved. But on this occasion the supervising General in command, the British War Office, and the Naval Transport Department all rose to a supreme degree of excellence in their arrangements. So too did the Railway Companies concerned. The details were meticulously correct. Without the loss of man, horse, or gun, the soldiers who had seen the sun set in Hampshire saw it rise in Picardy or in Normandy. Boulogne and Havre were the chief ports of disembarkation, but many, including the cavalry, went up the Seine and came ashore at Rouen. The soldiers everywhere received a rapturous welcome from the populace, which they returned by a cheerful sobriety of behaviour. The admirable precepts as to wine and women set forth in Lord Kitchener's parting orders to the Army seem to have been most scrupulously observed. It is no slight upon the gallantry of France – the very home of gallantry – if it be said that she profited greatly at this strained, over-anxious time by the arrival of these boisterous over-sea Allies. The tradition of British solemnity has been for ever killed by these jovial invaders. It is probable that the beautiful tune, and even the paltry words of "Tipperary," will pass into history as the marching song, and often the death-dirge, of that gallant host. The dusty, poplar-lined roads resounded with their choruses, and the quiet Picardy villages re-echoed their thunderous and superfluous assurances as to the state of their hearts. All France broke into a smile at the sight of them, and it was at a moment when a smile meant much to France.

Whilst the various brigades were with some deliberation preparing for an advance up-country, there arrived at the Gare du Nord in Paris a single traveller who may be said to have been the most welcome British visitor who ever set foot in the city. He was a short, thick man, tanned by an outdoor life, a solid, impassive personality with a strong, good-humoured face, the forehead of a thinker above it, and the jaw of an obstinate fighter below. Overhung brows shaded a pair of keen grey eyes, while the strong, set mouth was partly concealed by a grizzled moustache. Such was John French, leader of cavalry in Africa and now Field-Marshal commanding the Expeditionary Forces of Britain. His defence of Colesberg at a critical period when he bluffed the superior Boer forces, his dashing relief of Kimberley, and especially the gallant way in which he had thrown his exhausted cavalry across the path of Cronje's army in order to hold it while Roberts pinned it down at Paardeberg, were all exploits which were fresh in the public mind, and gave the soldiers confidence in their leader.

French might well appreciate the qualities of his immediate subordinates. Both of his army corps and his cavalry division were in good hands. Haig, like his leader, was a cavalry man by education, though now entrusted with the command of the First Army Corps, and destined for an ever-increasing European reputation. Fifty-four years of age, he still preserved all his natural energies, whilst he had behind him long years of varied military experience, including both the Soudanese and the South African campaigns, in both of which he had gained high distinction. He had the

John French, photographed in Paris.

advantage of thoroughly understanding the mind of his commander, as he had worked under him as Chief of the Staff in his remarkable operations round Colesberg in those gloomy days which opened the Boer War.

The Second Army Corps sustained a severe loss before ever it reached the field of action, for its commander, General Grierson, died suddenly of heart failure in the train between Havre and Rouen upon August 18. Grierson had been for many years Military Attaché in Berlin, and one can well imagine how often he had longed to measure British soldiers against the self-sufficient critics around him. At the very last moment the ambition of his lifetime was denied him. His place, however, was worthily filled by General Smith-Dorrien, another South African veteran whose brigade in that difficult campaign had been recognised as one of the very best. Smith-Dorrien was a typical Imperial soldier in the world-wide character of his service, for he had followed the flag, and occasionally preceded it, in Zululand, Egypt, the Soudan, Chitral, and the Tirah before the campaign against the Boers. A sportsman as well as a soldier, he had very particularly won the affections of the Aldershot division by his system of trusting to their honour rather than to compulsion in matters of discipline. It was seldom indeed that his confidence was abused.

Haig and Smith-Dorrien were the two generals upon whom the immediate operations were to devolve, for the Third Army Corps was late, through no fault of its own, in coming into line. There remained the Cavalry Division commanded by General Allenby, who was a column leader in that great class for mounted tactics held in South Africa a dozen years before. It is remarkable that of the four leaders in the initial operations of the German War – French, Smith-Dorrien, Haig, and Allenby – three belonged to the cavalry, an arm which has usually been regarded as active and ornamental rather than intellectual. Pulteney, the commander of the Third Army Corps, was a product of the Guards, a veteran of much service and a well-known heavy-game shot. Thus, neither of the more learned corps were represented among the higher commanders upon the actual field of battle, but brooding over the whole operations was the steadfast, untiring brain of Joffre, whilst across the water the silent Kitchener, remorseless as Destiny, moved the forces of the Empire to the front. The last word in each case lay with the sappers.

The general plan of campaign was naturally in the hands of General Joffre, since he was in command of far the greater portion of the Allied Force. It has been admitted in France that the original dispositions might be open to criticism, since a number of the French troops had engaged themselves in Alsace and Lorraine, to the weakening of the line of battle in the north, where the fate of Paris was to be decided. It is small profit to a nation to injure its rival ever so grievously in the toe when it is itself in imminent danger of being stabbed to the heart. A further change in plan had been caused by the intense sympathy felt both by the French and the British for the gallant Belgians, who had done so much and gained so many valuable days for the Allies. It was felt that it would be unchivalrous not to advance and do what was possible to relieve the intolerable pressure which was crushing them. It was resolved, therefore, to abandon the plan which had been formed, by which the Germans should be led as far as possible from their base, and to attack them at once. For this purpose the French Army changed its whole dispositions, which had been formed on the idea of an attack from the east, and advanced over the Belgian frontier, getting into touch with the enemy at Namur and Charleroi, so as to secure the passages of the Sambre. It was in fulfilling its part as the left of the Allied line that on August 18 and 19 the British troops began to move northwards into Belgium. The First Army Corps advanced through Le Nouvion, St. Remy, and Maubeuge to Kouveroy, which is a village upon the Mons-Chimay road. There it linked on to the right of the Second Corps, which had moved up to the line of the Condé-Mons Canal. On the morning of Sunday, August 23, all these troops were in position. The 5th Brigade of Cavalry (Chetwode's) lay out upon the right front at Binche, but the remainder of the cavalry was brought to a point about five miles behind the centre of the line, so as to be able to reinforce either flank. The first blood of the land campaign had been drawn upon August 22 outside Soignies, when a reconnoitring squadron of the 4th Dragoon Guards under Captain Hornby charged and overthrew a body of the 4th German Cuirassiers, bringing back some prisoners. The 20th Hussars had enjoyed a similar experience. It was a small but happy omen.

The First Army Corps held the space between Mons and Binche, which was soon contracted to Bray as the eastward limit. Close to Mons, where the attack was expected to break, since the town is a point of considerable strategic importance, there was a thickening of the line of defence. From that point the Third Division and the Fifth, in the order named, carried on the British formation down the length of the Mons-Condé Canal. The front of the Army covered nearly twenty miles, an excessive strain upon so small a force in the presence of a compact enemy. If one looks at the general dispositions, it becomes clear that Sir John French was preparing for an attack upon his right flank. From all his information the enemy was to the north and to the east of him, so that if they set about turning his position it must be from the Charleroi direction. Hence, his right wing was laid back at an angle to the rest of his line, and the only cavalry which he kept in advance was thrown out to Binche in front of this flank. The rest of the cavalry was on the day of battle drawn in behind the centre of the Army, but as danger began to develop upon the left flank it was sent across in that direction, so that on the morning of the 24th it was at Thulin, at the westward end of the line.

The line of the canal was a most tempting position to defend from Condé to Mons, for it ran as straight as a Roman road across the path of an invader. But it was very different at Mons itself. Here it formed a most awkward loop. A glance at the diagram will show this formation. It was impossible to leave it undefended, and yet troops who held it were evidently subjected to a flanking artillery Are from each side. The canal here was also crossed by at least three substantial road bridges and one railway bridge. This section of the defence was under the immediate direction of General Smith-Dorrien, who at once took steps to prepare a second line of defence, thrown back to the right rear of the town, so that if the canal were forced the British array would remain unbroken. The immediate care of this weak point in the position was committed to General Beauchamp Doran's 8th Brigade, consisting of the 2nd Royal Scots, 2nd Royal Irish, 4th Middlesex, and 1st Gordon Highlanders. On their left, occupying the village of Nimy and the western side of the peninsula, as well as the immediate front of Mons itself, was the 9th Brigade (Shaw's), containing the 4th Royal Fusiliers, the 1st Northumberland Fusiliers, and the 1st Royal Scots Fusiliers, together with the 1st Lincolns. To the left of this brigade, occupying the eastern end of the Mons-Condé line of canal, was Cuthbert's 13th Brigade, containing the 2nd Scottish Borderers, 2nd West Ridings, 1st West Kents, and 2nd Yorkshire Light Infantry. It was on these three brigades, and especially on the 8th and 9th, that the impact of the German army was destined to fall. Beyond them, scattered somewhat thinly along the line of the Mons-Condé Canal from the railway bridge west of St. Ghislain, were the two remaining brigades of the Fifth Division, the 14th (Rolt's) and the 15th (Gleichen's), the latter being in divisional reserve. Still farther to the west the head of the newly arrived 19th Brigade just touched the canal, and was itself in touch with

French cavalry at Condé. Sundry units of artillery and field hospitals had not yet come up, but otherwise the two corps were complete.

Having reached their ground, the troops, with no realisation of immediate danger, proceeded to make shallow trenches. Their bands had not been brought to the front, but the universal singing from one end of the line to the other showed that the men were in excellent spirits. Cheering news had come in from the cavalry, detachments of which, as already stated, had ridden out as far as Soignies, meeting advance patrols of the enemy and coming back with prisoners and trophies. The guns were drawn up in concealed positions within half a mile of the line of battle. All was now ready, and officers could be seen on every elevation peering northwards through their glasses for the first sign of the enemy. It was a broken country, with large patches of woodland and green spaces between. There were numerous slag-heaps from old mines, with here and there a factory and here and there a private dwelling, but the sappers had endeavoured in the short time to clear a field of fire for the infantry. In order to get this field of fire in so closely built a neighbourhood, several of the regiments, such as the West Kents of the 13th and the Cornwalls of the 14th Brigades, had to take their positions across the canal with bridges in their rear. Thrilling with anticipation, the men waited for their own first entrance upon the stupendous drama. They were already weary and footsore, for they had all done at least two days of forced marching, and the burden of the pack, the rifle, and the hundred and fifty rounds per man was no light one. They lay snugly in their trenches under the warm August sun and waited. It was a Sunday, and more than one have recorded in their letters how in that hour of tension their thoughts turned to the old home church and the mellow call of the village bells.

A hovering aeroplane had just slid down with the news that the roads from the north were alive with the advancing Germans, but the estimate of the aviator placed them at two corps and a division of cavalry. This coincided roughly with the accounts brought in by the scouts and, what was more important, with the forecast of General Joffre. Secure in the belief that he was flanked upon one side by the 5th French Army, and on the other by a screen of French cavalry, whilst his front was approached by a force not appreciably larger than his own. General French had no cause for uneasiness. Had his airmen taken a wider sweep to the north and west, or had the French commander among his many pressing preoccupations been able to give an earlier warning to his British colleague, the trenches would, no doubt, have been abandoned before a grey coat had appeared, and the whole Army brought swiftly to a position of strategical safety. Even now, as they waited expectantly for the enemy, a vast steel trap was closing up for their destruction.

Let us take a glance at what was going on over that northern horizon. The American Powell had seen something of the mighty right swing which was to end the combat. Invited to a conference with a German general who was pursuing the national policy of soothing the United States until her own turn should come round, Mr. Powell left Brussels and chanced to meet Von Kluck's legions upon their western and southerly trek. He describes with great force the effect upon his mind of those endless grey columns, all flowing in the same direction, double files of infantry on either side of the road, and endless guns, motor-cars, cavalry, and transport between. The men, as he describes them, were all in the prime of life, and equipped with everything which years of forethought could devise. He was dazed and awed by the tremendous procession, its majesty and its self-evident efficiency. It is no wonder, for he was looking at the chosen legions of the most wonderful army that the world had ever seen – an army which represented the last possible word on the material and mechanical side of war. High in the van a Taube aeroplane, like an embodiment of that black eagle which is the fitting emblem of a warlike and rapacious race, pointed the path for the German hordes.

A day or two before, two American correspondents, Mr. Irvin Cobb and Mr. Harding Davis, had seen the same great army as it streamed westwards through Louvain and Brussels. They graphically describe how for three consecutive days and the greater part of three nights they poured past, giving the impression of unconquerable energy and efficiency, young, enthusiastic, wonderfully equipped. "Either we shall go forward or we die. We do not expect to fall back ever. If the generals would let them, the men would run to Paris instead of walking there." So spoke one of the leaders of that huge invading host, the main part of which was now heading straight for the British line. A second part, unseen and unsuspected, were working round by Tournai to the west, hurrying hard to strike in upon the British flank and rear. The German is a great marcher as well as a great fighter, and the average rate of progress was little less than thirty miles a day.

It was after ten o'clock when scouting cavalry were observed falling back. Then the distant sound of a gun was heard, and a few seconds later a shell burst some hundreds of yards behind the British lines. The British guns one by one roared into action. A cloud of smoke rose along the line of the woods in front from the bursting shrapnel, but nothing could be seen of the German gunners. The defending guns were also well concealed. Here and there, from observation points upon buildings and slag-heaps, the controllers of the batteries were able to indicate targets and register hits unseen by the gunners themselves. The fire grew warmer and warmer as fresh batteries dashed up and unlimbered on either side. The noise was horrible, but no enemy had been seen by the infantry, and little damage done.

But now an ill-omened bird flew over the British lines. Far aloft across the deep blue sky skimmed the dark Taube, curved, turned, and sailed northwards again. It had marked the shells bursting beyond the trenches. In an instant, by some devilish cantrip of signal or wireless, it had set the range right. A rain of shells roared and crashed along the lines of the shallow trenches. The injuries were not yet numerous, but they were inexpressibly ghastly. Men who had hardly seen worse than a cut finger in their lives gazed with horror at the gross mutilations around them. "One dared not look sideways," said one of them. Stretcher-bearers bent and heaved while wet, limp forms were hoisted upwards by their comrades. Officers gave short, sharp words of encouragement or advice. The minutes seemed very long, and still the shells came raining down. The men shoved the five-fold clips down into their magazines and waited with weary patience. A senior officer peering over the end of a trench leaned tensely forward and rested his glasses upon the grassy edge. "They're coming!" he whispered to his neighbour. It ran from lip to lip along the line of crouching men. Heads were poked up here and there above the line of broken earth. Soon, in spite of the crashing shells overhead, there was a fringe of peering faces. And there at last in front of them was the German enemy. After all the centuries, Briton and Teuton faced each other at last for the test of battle.

A stylist among letter-writers has described that oncoming swarm as grey clouds drifting over green fields. They had deployed under cover whilst the batteries were preparing their path, and now over an extended front to the north-west of Mons they were breaking out from the woods and coming rapidly onwards. The men fidgeted with their triggers, but no order came to fire. The officers were gazing with professional interest and surprise at the German formations. Were these the tactics of the army which had claimed to be the most scientific in Europe? British observers had seen it in peace-time and had conjectured that it was a screen for some elaborate tactics held up for the day of battle. Yet here they were, advancing in what in old Soudan days used to be described as the twenty-acre formation, against the best riflemen in Europe. It was not even a shoulder to shoulder column, but a mere crowd, shredding out in the front and dense to the rear. There was nothing of the swiftly weaving lines, the rushes of alternate companies, the twinkle and flicker of a modern attack. It was mediaeval, and yet it was impressive also in its immediate display of numbers and the ponderous insistence of its onward flow. It was not many weeks before the stern lesson of war taught very different formations to those of the grand Kaiser manoeuvres.

The men, still fingering their triggers, gazed expectantly at their officers, who measured intently the distance of the approaching swarms. The Germans had already begun to fire in a desultory fashion. Shrapnel was bursting thickly along the head of their columns but they were coming steadily onwards. Suddenly a rolling wave of independent firing broke out from the British position. At some portions of the line the enemy were at eight hundred, at others at one thousand yards. The men, happy in having something definite to do, snuggled down earnestly to their work and fired swiftly but deliberately into the approaching mass. Rifles, machine-guns, and field-pieces were all roaring together, while the incessant crash of the shells overhead added to the infernal uproar. Men lost all sense of time as they thrust clip after clip into their rifles. The German swarms staggered on bravely under that leaden sleet. Then they halted, vacillated, and finally thinned, shredded out, and drifted backwards like a grey fog torn by a gale. The woods absorbed them once again, whilst the rain of shells upon the British trenches became thicker and more deadly.

There was a lull in the infantry attack, and the British, peering from their shelters, surveyed with a grim satisfaction the patches and smudges of grey which showed the effect of their fire. But the rest was not a long one. With fine courage the German battalions re-formed under the shelter of the trees, while fresh troops from the rear pushed forward to stiffen the shaken lines. "Hold your fire!" was the order that ran down the ranks. With the confidence bred of experience, the men waited and still waited, till the very features of the Germans could be distinguished. Then once more the deadly fire rippled down the line, the masses shredded and dissolved, and the fugitives hurried to the woods. Then came the pause under shell fire, and then once again the emergence of the infantry, the attack, the check, and the recoil. Such were the general characteristics of the action at Mons over a large portion of the British line – that portion which extended along the actual course of the canal.

It is not to be supposed, however, that there was a monotony of attack and defence over the whole of the British position. A large part of the force, including the whole of the First Army Corps, was threatened rather than seriously engaged, while the opposite end of the line was also out of the main track of the storm. It beat most dangerously, as had been foreseen, upon the troops to the immediate west and north of Mons, and especially upon those which defended the impossible peninsula formed by the loop of the canal.

There is a road which runs from Mons due north through the village of Nimy to Jurbise. The defences to the west of this road were in the hands of the 9th Brigade. The 4th Royal Fusiliers, with the Scots Fusiliers, were the particular battalions which held the trenches skirting this part of the peninsula, while half the Northumberland Fusiliers were on the straight canal to the westward. To the east of Nimy are three road-bridges – those of Nimy itself, Lock No.5, and Aubourg Station. All these three bridges were defended by the 4th Middlesex, who had made shallow trenches which commanded them. The Gordons were on their immediate right. The field of fire was much interfered with by the mines and buildings which faced them, so that at this point the Germans could get up unobserved to the very front. It has also been already explained that the German artillery could enfilade the peninsula from each side, making the defence most difficult. A rush of German troops came between eleven and twelve o'clock across the Aubourg Station Bridge. It was so screened up to the moment of the advance that neither the rifles nor the machine-guns of the Middlesex could stop it. It is an undoubted fact that this rush was preceded by a great crowd of women and children, through which the leading files of the Germans could hardly be seen. At the same time, or very shortly afterwards, the other two bridges were forced in a similar manner, but the Germans in all three cases as they reached the farther side were unable to make any rapid headway against the British fire, though they made the position untenable for the troops in trenches between the bridges. The whole of the 8th Brigade, supported by the 2nd Irish Rifles from McCracken's 7th Brigade, which had been held in reserve at Ciply, were now fully engaged, covering the retirement of the Middlesex and Gordons. At some points the firing between the two lines of infantry was across the breadth of a road. Two batteries of the 40th Artillery Brigade, which were facing the German attack at this point, were badly mauled, one of them, the 23rd R.F.A., losing its gun teams. Major Ingham succeeded in reconstituting his equipment and getting his guns away.

It is well to accentuate the fact that though this was the point of the most severe pressure there was never any disorderly retirement, and strong reserves were available had they been needed. The 8th Brigade, at the time of the general strategical withdrawal of the Army, made its arrangements in a methodical fashion, and General Doran kept his hold until after nightfall upon Bois la Haut, which was an elevation to the east of Mons from which the German artillery might have harassed the British retreat, since it commanded all the country to the south. The losses of the brigade had, however, been considerable, amounting to not less than three hundred and fifty in the case of the 4th Middlesex, many being killed or wounded in the defence, and some cut off in the trenches between the various bridge-heads. Majors Davey and Abell of the Middlesex were respectively wounded and killed, with thirteen other officers.

It has as already been said that the line of the 4th Royal Fusiliers extended along the western perimeter up to Nimy Road Bridge, where Colonel MacMahon's section ended and that of Colonel Hull, of the Middlesex Regiment, began. To the west of this point was the Nimy Railway Bridge, defended also by Captain Ashburner's company of the 4th Royal Fusiliers. This was assaulted early, and was held for nearly five hours against an attack of several German battalions. The British artillery was unable to help much in the defence, as the town of Mons behind offered no positions for guns, but the 107th Battery in the immediate rear did good work. The defence was continued until the Germans who had already crossed to the east were advancing on the flank. Lieutenant Maurice Dease, five times wounded before he was killed, worked his machine-gun to the end, and every man of his detachment was hit. Lieutenant Dease and Private Godley both received the Victoria Cross. The occupants of one trench, including Lieutenant Smith, who was wounded, were cut off by the rush. Captain Carey commanded the covering company and the retirement was conducted in good order, though Captain Bowden Smith, Lieutenant Mead, and a number of men fell in the movement. Altogether, the Royal Fusiliers lost five officers and about two hundred men in the defence of the bridge, Lieutenant Tower having seven survivors in his platoon of sixty. Captain Byng's company at the Glin Bridge farther east had severe losses and was driven in in the same way. As the infantry retired a small party of engineers under Captain Theodore Wright endeavoured to destroy this and other bridges, Lieutenant Day was twice wounded in his attempt upon the main Nimy Bridge. Corporal Jarvis received the V.C. for his exertions in preparing the Jemappes bridge for destruction to the west of Nimy. Captain Wright, with Sergeant Smith, made an heroic endeavour under terrific fire to detonate the charge, but was wounded and fell into the canal. Lieutenant Holt, a brave young officer of reserve engineers, also lost his life in these operations.

Having held on as long as was possible, the front line of the 9th Brigade fell back upon the prepared position on high ground between Mons and Frameries, where the 107th R.F.A. was entrenched. The 4th Royal Fusiliers passed through Mons and reached the new line in good order and without further loss. The 1st Royal Scots Fusiliers, however, falling back to the same point on a different route through Flénu, came under heavy machine-gun fire from a high soil heap, losing Captain Rose and a hundred men.

The falling back of the 8th and 9th Brigades from the Nimy Peninsula had an immediate effect upon Cuthbert's 13th Brigade, which was on their left holding the line up to the railway bridge just east of St. Ghislain. Of this brigade two battalions, the 1st West Kent on the right and the 2nd Scottish Borderers on the left, were in the trenches while the 2nd West Riding and the 2nd Yorkshire Light Infantry were in support, having their centre at Boussu. The day began by some losses to the West Kent Regiment, who were probably, apart from cavalry patrols, the first troops to suffer in the great war. A company of the regiment under Captain Lister was sent across the canal early as a support to some advancing cavalry, and was driven in about eleven o'clock with a loss of two officers and about a hundred men.

From this time onwards the German attacks were easily held, though the German guns were within twelve hundred yards. The situation was changed when it was learned later in the day that the Germans were across to the right and had got as far as Flénu on the flank of the brigade. In view of this advance. General Smith-Dorrien, having no immediate supports, dashed off on a motor to Sir Douglas Haig's headquarters some four miles distant, and got his permission to use Haking's 5th Brigade, which pushed up in time to re-establish the line.

It has been shown that the order of the regiments closely engaged in the front line was, counting from the east, the 1st Gordons, the 4th Middlesex, the 4th Royal Fusiliers, the 1st Scots Fusiliers, half the 1st Northumberland Fusiliers, the 1st West Kents, and the 2nd Scottish Borderers, the other regiments of these brigades being in reserve. The last-named battalion, being opposite a bridge, was heavily engaged all day, losing many men, but holding its position intact against repeated advances. On the left hand or western side of the Scottish Borderers, continuing the line along the canal, one would come upon the front of the 14th Brigade (Rolt's), which was formed by the 1st Surrey on the right and the 1st Duke of Cornwall's on the left. The German attack upon this portion of the line began about 1 P.M., and by 3 P.M. had become so warm that the reserve companies were drawn into the firing line. Thanks to their good work, both with rifles and with machine-guns, the regiments held their own until about six o'clock in the evening, when the retirement of the troops on their right enabled the Germans to enfilade the right section of the East Surreys at close range. They were ordered to retire, but lost touch with the left section, which remained to the north of the canal where their trench was situated. Captain Benson of this section had been killed and Captain Campbell severely wounded, but the party of one hundred and ten men under Lieutenant Morritt held on most gallantly and made a very fine defence. Being finally surrounded, they endeavoured to cut their way out with cold steel, Lieutenant Ward being killed and Morritt four times wounded in the attempt. Many of the men were killed and wounded, and the survivors were taken. Altogether the loss of the regiment was five officers and one hundred and thirty-four men.

On the left of the East Surreys, as already stated, lay the 1st Duke of Cornwall's of the same brigade. About four o'clock in the afternoon the presence of the German outflanking corps first made itself felt. At that hour the Cornwalls were aware of an advance upon their left as well as their front. The Cornwalls drew in across the canal in consequence, and the Germans did not follow them over that evening.

The chief point defended by the 14th Brigade upon this day had been the bridge and main road which crosses the canal between Pommeroeul and Thulin, some eight or nine miles west of Mons. In the evening, when the final order for retreat was given, this bridge was blown up, and the brigade fell back after nightfall as far as Dour, where it slept.

By the late afternoon the general position was grave, but not critical. The enemy had lost very heavily, while the men in the trenches were, in comparison, unscathed. Here and there, as we have seen, the Germans had obtained a lodgment in the British position, especially at the salient which had always appeared to be impossible to hold, but, on the other hand, the greater part of the Army, including the whole First Corps, had not yet been seriously engaged, and there were reserve troops in the immediate rear of the fighting line who could be trusted to make good any gap in the ranks before them. The German artillery fire was heavy and well-directed, but the British batteries had held their own. Such was the position when, about 5 P.M., a telegram from General Joffre was put into Sir John French's hand, which must have brought a pang to his heart. From it he learned that all his work had been in vain, and that far from contending for victory, he would be fortunate if he saved himself from utter defeat.

There were two pieces of information in this fatal message, and each was disastrous. The first announced that instead of the two German corps whom he had reason to think were in front of him, there were four – the Third, Fourth, Seventh, and Fourth Reserve Corps – forming, with the second and fourth cavalry divisions, a force of nearly 200,000 men, while the Second Corps were bringing another 40,000 round his left flank from the direction of Tournai. The second item was even more serious. Instead of being buttressed up with French troops on either side of him, he learned that the Germans had burst the line of the Sambre, and that the French armies on his right were already in full retreat, while nothing substantial lay upon his left. It was a most perilous position. The British force lay exposed and unsupported amid converging foes who far outnumbered it in men and guns. What was the profit of one day of successful defence if the morrow would dawn upon a British Sedan? There was only one course of action, and Sir John decided upon it in the instant, bitter as the decision must have been. The Army must be extricated from the battle and fall back until it resumed touch with its Allies.

But it is no easy matter to disengage so large an army which is actually in action and hard-pressed by a numerous and enterprising enemy. The front was extensive and the lines of retreat were limited. That the operation was carried out in an orderly fashion is a testimony to the skill of the General, the talents of the commanders, and the discipline of the units. If it had been done at once and simultaneously it would certainly have been the signal for a vigorous German advance and a possible disaster. The positions were therefore held, though no efforts were made to retake those points where the enemy had effected a lodgment. There was no possible use in wasting troops in regaining positions which would in no case be held. As dusk fell, a dusk which was lightened by the glare of burning villages, some of the regiments began slowly to draw off to the rear. In the early morning of the 24th the definite order to retire was conveyed to the corps commanders, whilst immediate measures were taken to withdraw the impedimenta and to clear the roads.

After a night of flames and of uproar the day dawned, a day of great anxiety to the British commanders and of considerable pressure upon a portion of the troops. Sir John French had given instructions that the First Corps, which had been only slightly engaged the day before, should pretend to assume the offensive upon the extreme right wing in the direction of Binche, whilst the Second Corps began its retirement. The enemy was following up rapidly, however, along the whole length of the British line, both flanks of which were exposed. Shortly after dawn the evacuated positions had been occupied, and Mons itself was in the hands of the advancing Germans. The Second Corps began its retreat, helped by the feint which was carried out by General Haig upon the right, and by the bulk of the batteries of both corps, but the pursuit was vigorous and the shell-fire incessant. A shell from the rear is more intimidating than twenty in the front. Hamilton's Third Division, including the 8th and 9th

Brigades, who had done such hard work the day before, sustained the most severe losses, especially at Frameries, four miles south of Mons. The 2nd Royal Scots of the 8th Brigade about midnight had been attacked by a heavy German column which got so near that the swish of their feet through the long grass put the regiment on the alert. The attack was blown back by a volley at close quarters. The 9th Brigade (Shaw's), which covered the retreat, was closely pressed from dawn by the pursuing Germans, and was subjected to a very heavy shell-fire. A barricade, erected in the village and manned by Captain Sandilands, of the Northumberlands, with his company, held up the German advance, and they were never permitted to reach the line nor to hustle the retirement. Butler's 23rd Artillery Brigade helped with its fire. The chief losses in this skilful covering action fell upon the 1st Lincolns and upon the 1st Northumberland Fusiliers, each of which lost about 150 men, including Captain Rose, Lieutenants Bulbe, Welchman, and others. There was a stational ambulance in the village of Frameries, and a foreign nurse in its employ has left a vivid picture of the wounded British rushing in grimy and breathless to have their slighter wounds dressed and then running out, rifle in hand, to find their place in the firing line.

The remaining brigade of the Third Division, McCracken's 7th Brigade, had detached one regiment, the 2nd Irish Rifles, upon the day before to reinforce the 8th Brigade, and this regiment had, as already mentioned, some severe fighting, holding back the German advance after the retirement from the Nimy Peninsula of the Middlesex and the Gordons. It did not find its way back to its brigade until the evening of the 24th. The brigade itself, during the first day of the retreat,, held a position near Ciply, to the south of Mons, where it was heavily attacked in the early morning, and in some danger as its flank was exposed. At ten o'clock it was ordered to retire via Genly towards Bavai, and it carried out this difficult movement in the face of a pushful enemy in perfect order, covered by the divisional artillery. The principal losses fell upon the 2nd South Lancashire Regiment, which came under heavy fire from German machine-guns posted upon slag-heaps. This regiment was very hard hit.

losing several hundred men. The brigade faced round near Bavai and held off the pursuit.

Cuthbert's 13th Brigade, keeping in line with their comrades on the right, halted at Wasmes, some four miles from the canal, where they prepared some hasty entrenchments. Here, at the dawn of day, they were furiously attacked by the German vanguard at the same time that the 9th Brigade was hustled in Frameries, but for two hours the assailants were beaten back with heavy losses. The brunt of the fighting fell upon the 2nd West Riding Regiment, who lost heavily, were at one time nearly surrounded, and finally, with dour Yorkshire pertinacity, shook themselves clear. Their losses included their commander. Colonel Gibbs, their adjutant, 300 men, and all their officers save five. The 1st West Kents also lost about 100 men and several officers, including Major Pack-Beresford. For the remainder of the day and for the whole of the 25th the brigade, with the rest of the Fifth Division, fell back with little fighting via Bavai to the Le Cateau line.

On the evening of the 23rd the 14th Brigade, still farther to the west, had fallen back to Dour, blowing up the bridge and road over the canal. After dark the Germans followed them, and Gleichen's 15th Brigade, which had not yet been engaged, found itself in the position of rearguard and immediately exposed to the pressure of the German flanking movement. This was now threatening to envelop the whole of Ferguson's Fifth Division. The situation was particularly difficult, since this General had to make a flank movement in the face of the enemy in order to close up with his comrades of the Third Division. He was soon compelled to call for assistance, and Allenby, with his cavalry division, was advanced to help him. It was evidently the intention of the enemy to strike in upon the western side of the division and pin it to its ground until it could be surrounded.

The first menacing advance in the morning of the 24th was directed against the flank of the British infantry who were streaming down the Elouges-Dour high-road. The situation was critical, and a portion of De Lisle' s 2nd Cavalry Brigade was ordered to charge near Andregnies, the hostile infantry being at that time about a thousand yards distant, with several batteries in support. The attack of the cavalry was vigorously supported by L Battery of Horse Artillery. The charge was carried out by three squadrons of the 9th Lancers, Colonel Campbell at their head. The 4th Dragoon Guards under Colonel Mullens was in support. The cavalry rode forward amidst a heavy but not particularly deadly fire until they were within a few hundred yards of the enemy, when, being faced by a wire fence, they swung to the right and rallied under the cover of some slag-heaps and of a railway embankment. Their menace and rifle fire, or the fine work of Major Sclater-Booth's battery, had the effect of holding up the German advance for some time, and though the cavalry were much scattered and disorganised they were able to reunite without any excessive loss, the total casualties being a little over two hundred. Some hours later the enemy's pressure again became heavy upon Ferguson's flank, and the 1st Cheshires and 1st Norfolks, of Gleichen's 15th Brigade, which formed the infantry flank-guard, incurred heavy losses. It was in this defensive action that the 119th R.F.A., under Major Alexander, fought itself to a standstill with only three unwounded gunners by the guns. The battery had silenced one German unit and was engaged with three others. Only Major Alexander and Lieutenant Pollard with a few men were left. As the horses had been destroyed the pieces had to be man-handled out of action. Captain the Hon. F. Grenfell, of the 9th Lancers, bleeding from two wounds, with several officers, Sergeants Davids and Turner, and some fifty men of the regiment, saved these guns under a terrible fire, the German infantry being within close range.

During the whole long, weary day the batteries and horsemen were working hard to cover the retreat, while the surgeons exposed themselves with great fearlessness, lingering behind the retiring lines in order to give first aid to the men who had been hit by the incessant shell-fire. It was in this noble task – the noblest surely within the whole range of warfare – that Captain Malcolm Leckie, and other brave medical officers, met with a glorious end, upholding to the full the traditions of their famous corps.

It is not to be supposed that so huge a force was all moving abreast, or available simultaneously at any one point. None the less a General can use his advance corps very much more freely when he knows that every gap can be speedily filled.

A tiny reinforcement had joined the Army on the morning after the battle of Mons. This was the 19th Brigade under General Drummond, which consisted of the 1st Middlesex, 1st Scots Rifles, 2nd Welsh Fusiliers, and 2nd Argyll and Sutherland Highlanders. This detached brigade acted, and continued to act during a large part of the war, as an independent unit. It detrained at Valenciennes on August 23, and two regiments, the Middlesex and the Cameronians, may be said to have taken part in the battle of Mons, since they formed up at the east of Condé, on the extreme left of the British position, and received, together with the Queen's Bays, who were scouting in front of them, the first impact of the German flanking corps. They fell back with the Army upon the 24th and 25th, keeping the line Jenlain – Solesmes, finally reaching Le Cateau, where they eventually took up their position on the right rear of the British Army.

As the Army fell back, the border fortress of Maubeuge with its heavy guns offered a tempting haven of rest for the weary and overmatched troops, but not in vain had France lost her army in Metz. Sir John French would have no such protection, however violently the Germans might push him towards it. "The British Army Invested in Maubeuge" was not destined to furnish the headline of a Berlin special edition. The fortress was left to the eastward, and the tired troops snatched a few hours of rest near Bavai, still pursued by the guns and the searchlights of their persistent foemen. At an early hour of the 25th the columns were again on the march for the south, and for safety.

It may be remarked that in all this movement what made the operation most difficult and complicated was, that in the retirement the Army was not moving direct to the rear, but diagonally away to the west, thus making the west flank more difficult to cover as well as complicating the movements of transport. It was this oblique movement which caused the

Third Division to change places with the Fifth, so that from now onwards it was to the west of the Army.

The greater part of the Fourth Division of the Third Army Corps, coming up from the lines of communication, brought upon this day a welcome reinforcement to the Army and did yeoman work in covering the retirement.

These troops, which had been quartered in the Ligny and Montigny area, received urgent orders at one in the morning of the 25th that they should advance northwards. They marched that night to Briastre, where they covered the retreat of the Army, the Third Division passing through their lines. The Fourth Division then retired south again, having great difficulty in getting along, as the roads were choked with transport and artillery, and fringed with exhausted men. The 12th Brigade (Wilson's) was acting as rearguard, and began to experience pressure from the pursuers, the Essex men being shelled out of the village of Bethencourt, which they held until it was nearly surrounded by the German cavalry. The line followed by the division was Briastre-Viesly-Bethencourt-Caudry-Ligny and Haucourt, the latter village marking the general position which they were to take up on the left of the Army at the line of Le Cateau. Such reinforcements were mere handfuls when compared with the pursuing hosts, but their advent heartened up the British troops and relieved them of some of the pressure. It has been remarked by officers of the Fourth Division that they and their men were considerably taken aback by the worn appearance of the weary regiments from Mons which passed through their ranks. Their confidence was revived, however, by the undisturbed demeanour of the General Headquarters Staff, who came through them in the late afternoon of the 25th. "General French himself struck me as being extremely composed, and the staff officers looked very cheerful." These are the imponderabilia which count for much in a campaign.

Tuesday, August 25, was a day of scattered rearguard actions. The weary Army had rested upon the evening of the 24th upon the general line Maubeuge -Bavai-Wargnies. Orders were issued for the retirement to continue next day to a position already partly prepared, in front of the centre of which stood the town of Le Cateau. All rearguards were to be clear of the above-mentioned line by 5:30 A.M. The general conception was that the inner flanks of the two corps should be directed upon Le Cateau.

The intention of the Commander-in-Chief was that the Army should fight in that position next day, the First Corps occupying the right and the Second Corps the left of the position. The night of the 25th found the Second Corps in the position named, whilst their comrades were still at Landrecies, eight miles to the north-east, with a cavalry brigade endeavouring to bridge the gap between. It is very certain, in the case of so ardent a leader as Haig, that it was no fault upon his part which kept him from Smith-Dorrien's side upon the day of battle. It can only be said that the inevitable delays upon the road experienced by the First Corps, including the rear-guard actions which it fought, prevented the ensuing battle from being one in which the British Army as a whole might have stemmed the rush of Von Kluck's invading host.

Whilst the whole Army had been falling back upon Solesmes, the position which had been selected for a stand, it was hoped that substantial French reinforcements were coming up from the south. The roads were much blocked during the 25th, for two divisions of French territorials were retiring along them, as well as the British Army. As a consequence progress was slow, and the German pressure from the rear became ever more severe. Allenby's cavalry and horse-guns covered the retreat, continually turning round and holding off the pursuers. Finally, near Solesmes, on the evening of the 25th, the cavalry were at last driven in, and the Germans came up against McCracken's 7th Brigade, who held them most skilfully until nightfall with the assistance of the 42nd Brigade R.F.A. and the 30th Howitzer Brigade. Most of the fighting fell upon the 1st Wiltshires and 2nd South Lancashires, both of which had substantial losses. The Germans could make no further progress, and time was given for the roads to clear and for the artillery to get away. The 7th Brigade then followed, marching, so far as possible, across country The Battle and taking up its position, which it did not reach until after midnight, in the village of Caudry, on the line of the Le Cateau – Courtrai road. As it faced north once more it found Snow's Fourth Division upon its left, while on its immediate right were the 8th and the 9th Brigades, with the Fifth Division on the farther side of them. One unit of the 7th Brigade, the 2nd Irish Rifles, together with the 41st R.F.A., swerved off in the darkness and confusion and went away with the cavalry. The rest were in the battle line. Here we may leave them in position while we return to trace the fortunes of the First Army Corps.

Sir Douglas Haig's corps, after the feint of August 24, in which the Second Division appeared to be attacking with the First in support, was cleverly disengaged from the enemy and fell back by alternate divisions. It was not an easy operation, and it was conducted under a very heavy shell-fire, which fell especially upon the covering guns of Colonel Sandilands' 34th Artillery Brigade. These guns were exposed to a concentration of fire from the enemy, which was so intense that a thick haze of smoke and dust blotted out the view for long periods at a time. It was only with difficulty and great gallantry that they were got away. An officer of the 6th Brigade, immediately behind them, writes: "Both going in and coming back the limbers passed my trench at a tearing gallop, the drivers lying low on the horses' necks and screaming at them to go faster, while on the return the guns bounded about on the stubble field like so many tin cans behind a runaway dog."

The guns having been drawn in, the corps retired by roads parallel to the Second Corps, and were able to reach the line Bavai – Maubeuge by about 7 P.M. upon that evening, being on the immediate eastern flank of Smith-Dorrien's men. It is a striking example of the historical continuity of the British Army that as they marched that day many of the regiments, such as the Guards and the 1st King's Liverpool, passed over the graves of their predecessors who had died under the same colours at Malplaquet in 1709, two hundred and six years before.

On August 25 General Haig continued his retreat. During the day he fell back to the west of Maubeuge by Feignies to Vavesnes and Landrecies.

The considerable forest of Mormal intervened between the two sections of the British Army. On the forenoon of this day the vanguard of the German infantry, using motor transport, overtook Davies' 6th Brigade, which was acting as rearguard to the corps. They pushed in to within five hundred yards, but were driven back by rifle-fire. Other German forces were coming rapidly up and enveloping the wings of the British rearguard, but the brigade, through swift and skilful handling, disengaged itself from what was rapidly becoming a dangerous situation. The weather was exceedingly hot during the day, and with their heavy packs the men were much exhausted, many of them being barely able to stagger. In the evening, footsore and weary, they reached the line of Landrecies, Maroilles, and Pont-sur-Sambre. The 4th Brigade of Guards, consisting of Grenadiers, Coldstream, and Irish, under General Scott-Kerr, occupied the town of Landrecies. During the day they had seen little of the enemy, and they had no reason to believe that the forest, which extended up to the outskirts of the town, was full of German infantry pressing eagerly to cut them off. The possession of vast numbers of motor lorries for infantry transport introduces a new element into strategy, especially the strategy of a pursuit, which was one of those disagreeable first experiences of up-to-date warfare which the British Army had to undergo. It ensures that the weary retreating rearguard shall ever have a perfectly fresh pursuing vanguard at its heels.

Dawn broke upon August 26, a day upon which the exhausted troops were destined to be tried to the limit of human endurance. It was the date of Von Kluck's exultant telegram in which he declared that he held them surrounded, a telegram which set Berlin fluttering with flags. On this day the First Army Corps was unmolested in its march, reaching the Venerolles line that night. There was woody country upon the west of it, and from beyond this curtain of trees they heard the distant roar of a terrific cannonade, and knew that a great battle was in progress to the westward. It was on Smith-Dorrien's Second Corps and upon the single division of the Third Corps that the full storm of the German attack had broken. In a word, a corps and a half of British troops, with 225 guns, were assailed by certainly four and probably five German corps, with 600 guns. It is no wonder that the premature tidings of a great German triumph were forwarded that morning to make one more item in that flood of good news which from August 21 to the end of the month was pouring in upon the German people. A glittering mirage lay before them. The French lines had been hurled back from the frontier, the British were in full retreat, and now were faced with absolute disaster. Behind these breaking lines lay the precious capital, the brain and heart of France. But God is not always with the big battalions, and the end was not yet.

Wounded soldiers from the Battle of Mons.

The Battle of Le Cateau

REFERENCE has already been made to the retirement of Smith-Dorrien's Second Corps, covered by Allenby's cavalry, throughout the 25th. The heads of columns arrived at the Le Cateau position at about 3 P.M., but the rearguards were fighting into the night, and came in eventually in an exhausted condition. The Fourth Division, which was still quite fresh, did good and indeed vital service by allowing the tired units to pass through its ranks and acting as a pivot upon which the cavalry could fall back.

Sir John French had reconsidered the idea of making a stand at Le Cateau, feeling, no doubt, that if his whole Army could not be consolidated there the affair would be too desperate. He had moved with his staff during the evening of the 25th to St. Quentin, leaving word that the retirement should be continued early next morning. Smith-Dorrien spent the afternoon and evening going round the position, but it was not until 2 A.M. upon the morning of the 26th that he was able to ascertain the whereabouts of all his scattered and weary units. About that time General Allenby reported that his cavalry had been widely separated, two and a half brigades being at Chatillon, six miles east of Le Cateau, the other one and a half brigades being near Ligny, four miles west of the same town. General Smith-Dorrien was in the position that his troops were scattered, weary, and in danger of losing their morale through continued retreat in the presence of an ever-pressing enemy. Even with the best soldiers such an experience too long continued may turn an army into a rabble. He therefore made urgent representations by telephone to the Commander-in-Chief, pointing out that the only hope of checking the dangerous German pursuit was to stagger them by a severe counter.

"The only thing for the men to do when they can't stand is to lie down and fight," said he. Sir John assented to the view, with the proviso that the retirement should be continued as soon as possible. Smith-Dorrien, taking under his orders the cavalry, the Fourth Division, and the 19th Brigade, as well as his own corps, issued instructions for the battle which he knew must begin within a few hours.

Owing to the gap of eight miles between the nearest points of the two corps, both flanks of the position were in the air. Smith-Dorrien therefore requested the cavalry brigades from Chatillon to move in and guard the east flank, while the rest of the cavalry watched the west. He was less anxious about the latter, as he knew that Sordet's French cavalry was in that direction.

The exhausted infantry, who had now been marching for about a week, and fighting for three days and the greater part of three nights, flung themselves down where best they could, some to the north-east of Le Cateau, some in the town, and some along the line of very inadequate trenches hastily prepared by civilian labour. In the early dawn they took up their position, the Fifth Division being to the right near the town. Of this division, the 14th Brigade (Rolt's) was on the extreme right, the 13th (Cuthbert's) to the left of it, and the 15th (Gleichen's) to the left again. To the west of the Fifth Division lay the Third, their trenches covering the villages of Troisville (9th Brigade), Audencourt (8th Brigade), and Caudry (7th Brigade). Behind Caudry one and a half brigades of cavalry were in reserve to strengthen the left wing. From Caudry the line was thrown back to meet a flanking movement and extended to Haucourt. This portion was held by Snow's Fourth Division. Sordet's cavalry had passed across the rear of the British position the day before, and lay now to the left flank and rear of the Army. There were rumours of approaching French forces from the south, which put heart into the weary men, but, as a matter of fact, they had only their own brave spirits upon which to depend. Their numbers, putting every unit at its full complement, were about 70,000 men. Their opponents were four army corps at the least, with two divisions of cavalry – say, 170,000 men with an overpowering artillery. Subsequent reports showed that the guns of all five army corps had been concentrated for the battle.

It has been said that Rolt's 14th Brigade was at the extreme right of the line. This statement needs some expansion. The 14th Brigade consisted of the 1st East Surrey, 2nd Suffolk, 2nd Manchester, and 1st Cornwalls. Of these four regiments, half of the East Surrey had been detached on escort duty and the other half, under Colonel Longley, with the whole of the Cornwalls, bivouacked in the northern suburbs of Le Cateau on the night of the 25th. In the early morning of the 26th the enemy's advanced guard got into the town, and this detachment of British troops were cut off from their comrades and fired upon as they assembled in the streets of the town. They made their way out, however, in orderly fashion and took up a position to the south-east of the town, where they fought an action on their own account for some hours, quite apart from the rest of the Army, which they could hear but not see. Eventually the division of cavalry fell back from Chatillon to join the Army and picked up these troops en route, so that the united body was able to make its way safely back to their comrades. These troops were out of the main battle, but did good work in covering the retreat. The whole signal section of the 14th Brigade was with them, which greatly hampered the brigade during the battle. Two companies of the 1st East Surreys under Major Tew had become separated from their comrades after Mons, but they rejoined the British line at Troisville, and on the morning of August 26 were able to fall in on the rear of the 14th Brigade, where, as will be seen later, they did good service.

The 19th Brigade had also bivouacked in Le Cateau and was nearly cut off, as the two regiments of the 14th Brigade had been, by the sudden intrusion of the enemy. It had been able to make its way out of the town, however, without being separated from the rest of the Army, and it took up its position on the right rear of the infantry line, whence it sent help where needed and played the part of a reserve until towards the close of the action its presence became very vital to the Fifth Division. At the outset the 2nd Argyll and Sutherlands were in the front line of this brigade and the 1st Middlesex supporting them, while the other two battalions, the 2nd Welsh Fusiliers and 1st Scots Rifles, with a battery of artillery had been taken as a reserve by the force commander. No trenches had been prepared at this point, and the losses of the two front battalions from shell-fire were, from the beginning, very heavy. The other two battalions spent a day of marching rather than fighting, being sent right across to reinforce the Fourth Division and then being brought back to the right flank once more.

It was the Fifth Division, on the right of the line, who first experienced the full effect of the heavy shelling which about seven o'clock became general along the whole position, but was always most severe upon the right. There was a dangerous salient in the trenches at the cross-roads one mile west of Le Cateau which was a source of very great weakness. Every effort was made to strengthen the trenches, the 15th Brigade and 59th Company R.E. working especially hard in the Troisville section. The Germans were moving round upon this right wing, and the murderous hail of missiles came from the flank as well as from the front, being supplemented by rifle and machine-gun fire. The 2nd Suffoiks and 2nd Manchesters, the remaining half of Rolt's 14th Brigade, being on the extreme right of the line, suffered the most. The guns immediately supporting them, of the 28th Artillery Brigade, were quite overmatched and were overwhelmed by the devastating rain of shells, many of them being put out of action. A heavy battery, The Battle the 108th, some little distance behind the line, kept Le Cateau. up a steady and effective fire which long held back the German advance. The pressure, however, was extreme, and growing steadily from hour to hour until it became well-nigh intolerable. Especially it fell upon the 2nd Suffolks, who held their shallow trenches with splendid tenacity. Their colonel, Brett, was killed. Major Doughty was wounded in three places, Captains Orford and Cutbill, with eight lieutenants, were on the ground. Finally, when the position of the brigade became untenable and it was ordered to retreat, the gallant Suffolks held on to their line with the desire of saving the disabled guns, and were eventually all killed, wounded, or taken, save for about 250 men, while their neighbours, the 2nd Manchesters, lost 14 officers and 350 of their men. In this way the extreme right of the British line was practically destroyed.

The 19th Brigade, in the rear of the 14th, were able to observe the fate of their comrades, and about midday the 2nd Argyll and Sutherland Highlanders, who had already lost a good many men from shell-fire, advanced in the chivalrous hope of relieving the pressure. The battalion went forward as if on parade, though the casualties were numerous. They eventually gained the shelter of some trenches near the remains of the 14th Brigade, but their gallant effort, instead of averting the threatened destruction, ended by partially involving them in the same fate. They could do nothing against the concentrated and well-directed artillery fire of the enemy. When eventually they fell back, part of two companies were cut off in their trench and taken. The rest of the regiment, together with the 1st Middlesex and two companies of the Royal Scots Fusiliers from the 9th Brigade, formed a covering line on a ridge in the rear and held back the German advance for a long time. This line did not retire until 5 P.M., when it was nearly enveloped. General Drummond, commanding the 19th Brigade, had met with an injury in the course of the action, and it was commanded during the latter part by Colonel Ward, of the Middlesex.

The retirement or destruction of the 14th Brigade exposed the flank of the 13th (Cuthbert's) to murderous enfilade fire, which fell chiefly upon the 2nd Yorkshire Light Infantry. This brigade had defended itself successfully for six hours against various frontal attacks, but now the flank-fire raked it from end to end and practically destroyed the Yorkshiremen, who were the most exposed to it. On them and on the 2nd Scottish Borderers fell the great bulk of the losses, for the West Kents and the survivors of the West Ridings were in reserve. Of the two companies of the Yorkshire Light Infantry who held the foremost trenches, that on the right had only fifteen men left, with whom Major Yate attempted a final charge, finding his Victoria Cross in the effort, while the next company, under Major Trevor, had only forty-one survivors, the whole losses of the battalion being 600 men, with 20 officers. Both the Yorkshire and the Scottish Border battalions lost their colonels in the action. Their losses were shared by the two companies of the 1st East Surreys under Major Tew, who had been placed between the 14th and 13th Brigades, and who fought very steadily in shallow trenches, holding on to the last possible moment.

Whilst the battle was going badly on the right, the Third Division in the centre and the Fourth Division on the left had held their own against a succession of attacks. The 8th and 9th Brigades drove off the German infantry with their crushing rifle-fire, and endured as best they might the shelling, which was formidable and yet very much less severe than that to which the Fifth Division had been exposed. In the case of the 7th Brigade (McCracken's) the village of Caudry, which it defended, formed a salient, since the Fourth Division on the left was thrown back. The attack upon this brigade from daylight onwards was very severe, but the assailants could neither drive in the line nor capture the village of Caudry. They attacked on both flanks at short rifle range, inflicting and also enduring heavy losses. In this part of the field the British guns held their own easily against the German, the proportion of numbers being more equal than on the right of the line.

Whilst the right flank was crumbling before the terrific concentration of German guns, and while the centre was stoutly holding its own, farther to the west, in the Haucourt – Ligny direction, the Second German Army Corps was beating hard against Snow's Fourth Division, which was thrown back to protect the left flank of the Army, and to cover the Cambrai-Esnes road. Hunter-Weston's 11th Brigade was on the right, south of Fontaine, with Wilson's 12th upon its left, and Haldane's 10th in reserve at Haucourt. As the German attack came from the left, or western flank, the 12th Brigade received the first impact. The artillery of the division had not yet come up, and the 1st Royal Lancasters, stretched in a turnip patch, endured for some time a severe fire which cost them many casualties, including their Colonel Dykes, and to which little reply could be made. There were no cavalry scouts in front of the infantry, so that working parties and advanced posts were cut up by sudden machine-gun fire. Some of the covering parties both of the Lancasters and of the 2nd Lancashire Fusiliers were never seen again. At about seven the British guns came up, the 14th Brigade R.F.A. on the left, the 29th in the centre, and the 32nd on the right, with the howitzers of the 37th behind the right centre on the high ground near Selvigny. From this time onward they supported the infantry in the most self-sacrificing way. The German infantry advance began shortly afterwards, and was carried out by wave after wave of men. A company of the 2nd Essex Regiment, under Captain Vandeleur, upon the British left, having good cover and a clear field of fire, inflicted very heavy losses on the Germans, though they were finally overwhelmed, their leader having been killed. The 2nd Lancashire Fusiliers in the front line were also heavily attacked, and held their own for several hours. About ten o'clock the pressure was so great that the defence was driven in, and two battalions lost their machine-guns, but a new line was formed in the Haucourt-Esnes road, the retirement being skilfully covered by Colonel Anley, of the Essex, and Colonel Griffin, of the Lancashire Fusiliers. There the 2nd Inniskilling Fusiliers, the 1st Royal Lancasters, the 2nd Lancashire Fusiliers, and the 2nd Essex held firmly on until the afternoon under very heavy and incessant fire, while the 11th Brigade upon their right were equally involved in the fight. Two battalions of the 10th Brigade (Haldane's), the 1st Irish Fusiliers and 2nd Seaforths, had dug themselves in on the high ground just north of Selvigny and repulsed every attack, but two others, the 2nd Dublins and 1st Warwicks, had got involved with the 12th Brigade and could not be retrieved. The Signal Corps had not yet arrived, and the result was that General Snow had the greatest difficulty in ensuring his connections with his brigadiers, the orders being carried by his staff officers. At two o'clock, as there was a lull in the German advance, Wilson of the 12th Brigade made a spirited counter-attack, recovering many of the wounded, but being finally driven back to the old position by intense artillery and machine-gun fire.

It is worth recording that during this advance the Essex men found among the German dead many with the same Gibraltar badge upon their caps which they bore themselves. It was a Hanoverian battalion who had been comrades with the old 56th in the defence of the fortress one hundred and fifty years before.

The 11th Brigade (Hunter-Weston), on the right of the 12th, had meanwhile played a very vital part in the fight. This brigade was defending a position called Les Carrières, or the quarry pits, which was east of Fontaine and to the north of the village of Ligny. It was a desperate business, for the British were four times driven out of it and four times came back to their bitter work amid a sleet of shells and bullets. Parties of the 1st Somersets and of the 1st East Lancashires held the quarries with the 1st Hants and 1st Rifle Brigade in immediate support, all being eventually drawn into the fight. Major Rickman, of the latter regiment, distinguished himself greatly in the defence, but was seriously wounded and left behind in the final retirement. Besides incessant gun-fire, the defenders were under infantry fire of a very murderous description from both flanks. In spite of this, the place was held for six hours until the retirement of the line in the afternoon caused it to be untenable, as the enemy was able to get behind it. The brigade then fell back upon Ligny under heavy shrapnel-fire, moving steadily and in good order. The Germans at once attacked the village from the east and north-east. Could they have taken it, they would have been upon the flank of the British line of retirement. They were twice driven back, however, by the fire of the infantry, losing very heavily upon both occasions. About four o'clock, the Army being in full retreat, the brigade received orders to abandon Ligny and march upon Malincourt. The effect of a heavy shrapnel-fire was minimised by this movement being carried out in small columns of fours. A loss of 30 officers and 1115 men in a single day's fighting showed how severe had been the work of Hunter-Weston's brigade. The 12th Brigade had also lost about a thousand men. Many of the guns had run short of shells. A spectator has described how he saw the British gunners under a heavy fire, sitting in gloomy groups round the guns which they had neither the shells to work, nor the heart to abandon.

Such was the general fortune of the British left. At the extreme edge of it, in the gap between the left of the Fourth Division and the town of Cambrai, Sordet's French cavalry had been fighting to prevent the British wing from being turned. There was some misconception upon this point at the time, but in justice to our Ally it should be known that General Smith-Dorrien himself galloped to this flank in the course of the afternoon and was a witness of the efforts of the French troopers, who had actually marched 40 miles in order to be present at the battle.

The narrative has now taken the movements of the left wing up to the point of its retirement, in order to preserve the continuity of events in that portion of the field, but the actual abandonment of their position by Snow's Fourth Division was due to circumstances over which they had no control, and which had occurred at a considerable distance. Both the centre and the left of the Army could have held its own, though it must be admitted that the attack to which they were exposed was a very violent one gallantly pushed home.

All might have gone well had the Germans not been able to mass such an overpowering artillery attack upon the right of the line. It was shortly after mid-day that this part of the position began to weaken, and observers from the centre saw stragglers retiring over the low hill in the Le Cateau direction. At that hour the artillery upon the right of the British line was mostly silenced, and large masses of the German infantry were observed moving round the right flank. The salient of the Suffolks was in the possession of the enemy, and from it they could enfilade the line. It was no longer possible to bring up ammunition or horses to the few remaining guns. The greater part of the troops held on none the less most doggedly to their positions, A steady downpour of rain was a help rather than a discomfort, as it enabled the men to moisten their parched lips. But the situation of the Fifth Division was growing desperate. It was plain that to remain where they were could only mean destruction. And yet to ask the exhausted men to retire under such a rain of shells would be a dangerous operation. Even the best troops may reach their snapping point. Most of them had by the afternoon been under constant shrapnel-fire for eight hours on end. Some were visibly weakening. Anxious officers looked eagerly over their shoulders for any sign of reinforcement, but an impassable gap separated them from their comrades of the First Army Corps, who were listening with sinking hearts to the rumble of the distant cannonade. There was nothing for it but to chance the retirement. About three o'clock commanders called to officers and officers to men for a last great effort. It was the moment when a leader reaps in war the love and confidence which he has sown in peace. Smith-Dorrien had sent his meagre reserve, which consisted of one battery and two battalions, to take up a rearguard position astride the Le Cateau-St. Quentin road. Every available detail, that could pull a trigger, down to Hildebrand's signallers of the Headquarters Staff, who had already done wonderful work in their own particular line, were thrust into the covering line. One by one the dishevelled brigades were drawn off towards the south. One section of the heavy guns of the 108th Heavy Battery was ordered back to act with two battalions of the 19th Brigade in covering the Reumont-Maritz road, while the 1st Norfolks were put in echelon behind the right flank for the same purpose.

The Fifth Division, with the 15th Brigade as rearguard, considerably disorganised by its long hammering, retreated along the straight Roman road via Maritz and Estrées. The Third Division fell back through Berthy and Clary to Beaurevoir, the 9th Brigade forming a rearguard. The cavalry, greatly helped by Sordet's French cavalry upon the west, flung itself in front of the pursuit, while the guns sacrificed themselves to save the retiring infantry. Every British battery was an inferno of bursting shells, and yet every one fought on while breech-block would shut or gunner could stand. Many batteries were in the state of the 61st R.F.A., which fired away all its own shells and then borrowed from the limbers of other neighbouring batteries, the guns of which had been put out of action. Had the artillery gone the Army would have gone. Had the Army gone the Germans had a clear run into Paris. It has been said that on the covering batteries of Wing, Milne, and Headlam may, on that wet August afternoon, have hung the future history of Europe.

Wing's command included the 23rd, 30th, 40th, and 42nd Brigades, with the 48th Heavy Battery; Headlam's were the 15th, 27th, 28th, and 8th, with the 108th Heavy; Milne's, the 14th, 29th, 32nd, and 37th, with the 31st Heavy. These numbers deserve to be recorded, for every gun of them did great service, though many were left in ruins on the field. Some, like those of the 37th R.F.A., were plucked from under the very noses of the Germans, who were within a hundred yards of them when they were withdrawn, a deed of valour for which Captain Reynolds of that battery received the Cross. One by one those batteries which could move were drawn off, the cavalry covering the manoeuvre by their rifle-fire, and sometimes man-handling the gun from the field. Serving one day as charging cavaliers, another as mounted infantry in covering a retreat, again as sappers in making or holding a trench, or when occasion called for it as gun-teams to pull on the trace of a derelict gun, the cavalry have been the general utility men of the Army. The days of pure cavalry may have passed, but there will never be a time when a brave and handy fighting man who is mobile will not be invaluable to his comrades.

It was about four o'clock that the Fourth Division, on the left flank, who had been maintaining the successful defensive already described, were ordered to begin their retirement. The 12th Brigade was able to withdraw with no great difficulty along the line Walincourt-Villiers-Vendhuile, reaching the latter village about nine-thirty. The doings of the 11th Brigade have been already described. There was considerable disintegration but no loss of spirit. One of the regiments of the 12th, the 2nd Royal Lancasters, together with about three hundred Warwicks, from the 10th Brigade, and some detachments of other regiments, were by some mischance, isolated in the village of Haucourt with no definite orders, and held on until ten o'clock at night, when the place was nearly surrounded. They fought their way out, however, in a most surprising fashion, and eventually made good their retreat. One party, under Major Poole of the Warwicks, rejoined the Army next day. Captain Clutterbuck, with a small party of Royal Lancasters, wandered into Haumont after it was occupied by the Germans. Summoned to surrender the gallant officer refused, and was shot dead, but his men charged with the bayonet and fought their way clear to a post which was held by Major Parker of the same regiment, to the immediate south of the village. This officer, finding that he was the last rearguard, withdrew in the face of heavy German forces. Being joined by

Major Christie of the Warwicks with 200 men, they followed the Army, and, finally, by a mixture of good luck and good leadership, picked their way through the German advance guards, and on the third day rejoined the colours at Noyon.

Haldane's 10th Brigade had got split up during the confused fighting of the day, half of it, the 1st Warwicks and 2nd Dublins, getting involved with the 12th Brigade in the fighting on the Haucourt Ridge. The other two battalions, the 2nd Seaforths and 1st Royal Irish Fusiliers, kept guard as a reserve over the left flank of the division. Towards evening General Haldane, finding it hopeless to recover control of his lost regiments, collected the rest of his brigade, and endeavoured to follow the general line of retreat. He lost touch with the remainder of the Army, and might well have been cut off, but after a most exhausting experience he succeeded in safely rejoining the division at Roisel upon the 27th. It may be said generally that the reassembling of the Fourth Division after the disintegration they had experienced was a remarkable example of individualism and determination.

It is impossible to doubt that the Germans, in spite of their preponderating numbers, were staggered by the resistance which they had encountered. In no other way can one explain the fact that their pursuit, which for three days had been incessant, should now, at the most critical instant, have eased off. The cavalry and guns staved off the final blow, and the stricken infantry staggered from the field. The strain upon the infantry of the Fifth Division may be gathered from the fact that up to this point they had lost, roughly, 143 officers, while the Third Division had lost 92 and the Fourth 70. For the time they were disorganised as bodies, even while they preserved their morale as individuals.

When extended formations are drawn rapidly in under the conditions of a heavy action, it is often impossible to convey the orders to men in outlying positions. Staying in their trenches and unconscious of the departure of their comrades, they are sometimes gathered up by the advancing enemy, but more frequently fall into the ranks of some other corps, and remain for days or weeks away from their own battalion, turning up long after they have helped to swell some list of casualties. Regiments get intermingled and pour along the roads in a confusion which might suggest a rout, whilst each single soldier is actually doing his best to recover his corps. It is disorganisation – but not demoralisation.

It has been remarked above that in the widespread formations of modern battles it is difficult to be sure of the transmission of orders. An illustration of such a danger occurred upon this occasion, which gave rise to an aftermath of battle nearly as disastrous as the battle itself. This was the episode which culminated in the loss of a body of troops, including a large portion of the 1st Gordon Highlanders. This distinguished corps had been engaged with the rest of Beauchamp Doran's 8th Brigade at Mons and again upon the following day, after which they retreated with the rest of their division. On the evening of the 25th they bivouacked in the village of Audencourt, just south of the Cambrai – Le Cateau highway, and on the morning of the 26th they found themselves defending a line of trenches in front of this village. From nine o'clock the Gordons held their ground against a persistent German attack. About 3:30 an order was given for the battalion to retire. This message only reached one company, which acted upon it, but the messenger was wounded en route, and failed to reach battalion headquarters. Consequently the remainder of the battalion did not retire with the Army, but continued to hold its trenches, greatly helped by the flank (D) Company of Royal Scots, until long after nightfall, when the enemy in great force had worked round both of its flanks. It should be understood that the withdrawal of the Royal Scots was under direct order emanating from brigade headquarters, but an officer of the Gordons, not knowing that such an order had been issued, and perceiving that their flank would be exposed if D Company left their trench, said a few words to them which had such an effect upon their fiery souls that they rushed back to stand by the Highlanders, their Captain being shot dead as he waved his men back into their trench. From that time onwards this company of Royal Scots, finely led by two young lieutenants, Graves and Graham Watson, shared all the dangers and the ultimate fate of the Gordons, as did a handful of Royal Irish upon the other flank. When it was dusk it became clear to

Colonel Gordon, who was now in command of the mixed detachment, that he and his men were separated from the Army and surrounded on every side by the advancing Germans. At that time the men, after supreme exertion for several days, had been in action for twelve hours on end. He therefore decided, as against annihilation in the morning, that retreat was the only course open. The wounded were left in the trenches. The transport, machine-guns, and horses had already been destroyed by the incessant shelling. The detachment made a move towards the south, the operation being a most difficult one in pitch darkness with the enemy within a few hundred yards. The success attained in this initial stage was largely due to the way in which the Master of Saltoim conveyed the orders which drew in the flanks to the centre. Having made good the Audencourt-Caudry road at 1 A.M. on August 27, the troops managed to traverse some miles of road, with blazing villages all about them, and had a fair chance of reaching safety when unfortunately at Montigny they took a wrong turn, which brought them into Bertry which was held by the Germans. Some confusion was caused by the latter challenging in French. A confused fight followed in the darkness, in the course of which many individual acts of great bravery and devotion were performed. The enemy were now all round the Highlanders, and though the struggle continued for fifty minutes, and there was no official surrender, the little body of men was embedded in Von Kluck's army, and no escape could be found. The utmost discipline and gallantry were shown by all ranks. It must be some consolation to the survivors to know that it is freely admitted that their resistance in the trenches for so long a period undoubtedly facilitated the safe withdrawal of the Third, and to some extent of the Fourth Divisions. Major Leslie Butler, Brigade-Major of the 8th Brigade, who had made a gallant effort to ride to the Gordons and warn them of their danger, was entangled among the Germans, and only succeeded six days later in regaining the British lines.

So ended the perilous, costly, and almost disastrous action of Le Cateau. The loss to the British Army, so far as it can be extracted from complex figures and separated from the other losses of the retreat, amounted to between seven and eight thousand killed, wounded, and missing, while at the time of the action, or in the immediate retreat, a considerable quantity of transport and thirty-six field-pieces, mostly in splinters, were abandoned to the enemy. It was an action which could hardly have been avoided, and from which the troops were extricated on better terms than might have been expected. It will always remain an interesting academic question what would have occurred had it been possible for the First Corps to line up with the rest of the Army. The enemy's preponderance of artillery would probably have prevented a British victory, and the strategic position would in any case have made it a barren one, but at least the Germans would have been hard hit and the subsequent retreat more leisurely. As it stood, it was an engagement upon which the weaker side can look back without shame or dishonour. One result of it was to give both the Army and the country increased confidence in themselves and their leaders. Sir John French has testified to the splendid qualities shown by the troops, while his whole-hearted tribute to Smith-Dorrien, in which he said, "The saving of the left wing of the Army could never have been accomplished unless a commander of rare and unusual coolness, intrepidity, and determination had been Chapter present to personally conduct the operation," will surely be endorsed by history.

General Smith-Dorrien.

It is difficult to exaggerate the strain which had been thrown upon this commander. On him had fallen the immediate direction of the action at Mons; on him also had been the incessant responsibility of the retreat. He had, as has been shown in the narrative, been hard at work all night upon the eve of the battle; he superintended that trying engagement, he extricated his forces, and finally motored to St. Quentin in the evening, went on to Noyon, reached it after midnight, and was back with his Army in the morning, encouraging every one by the magnetism of his presence. It was a very remarkable feat of endurance.

Exhausted as the troops were, there could be no halt or rest until they had extricated themselves from the immediate danger. At the last point of human endurance they still staggered on through the evening and the night time, amid roaring thunder and flashing lightning, down the St. Quentin road. Many fell from fatigue, and having fallen, continued to sleep in ditches by the roadside, oblivious of the racket around them. A number never woke until they found themselves in the hands of the Uhlan patrols. Others slumbered until their corps had disappeared, and then, regaining their senses, joined with other straggling units so as to form bands, which wandered over the country, and eventually reached the railway line about Amiens with wondrous Bill Adams tales of personal adventures which in time reached England, and gave the impression of complete disaster. But the main body were, as a matter of fact, holding well together, though the units of infantry had become considerably mixed and so reduced that at least four brigades, after less than a week of war, had lost 50 per cent of their personnel. Many of the men threw away the heavier contents of their packs, and others abandoned the packs themselves, so that the pursuing Germans had every evidence of a rout before their eyes. It was deplorable that equipment should be discarded, but often it was the only possible thing to do, for either the man had to be sacrificed or the pack. Advantage was taken of a forked road to station an officer there who called out, "Third Division right. Fifth Division left," which greatly helped the reorganisation. The troops snatched a few hours of rest at St. Quentin, and then in the breaking dawn pushed upon their weary road once more, country carts being in many cases commandeered to carry the lame and often bootless infantry. The paved chaussées, with their uneven stones, knocked the feet to pieces, and caused much distress to the tired men, which was increased by the extreme heat of the weather.

In the case of some of the men the collapse was so complete that it was almost impossible to get them on. Major Tom Bridges, of the 4th Royal Irish Dragoons, being sent to round up and hurry forward 250 stragglers at St. Quentin, found them nearly comatose with fatigue. With quick wit he bought a toy drum, and, accompanied by a man with a penny whistle, he fell them in and marched them, laughing in all their misery, down the high road towards Ham. When he stopped he found that his strange following stopped also, so he was compelled to march and play the whole way to Roupy. Thus by one man's compelling personality 250 men were saved for the Army. But such complete collapse was rare. The men kept their morale. "Beneath the dirt and grime and weariness I saw clear eyes and grim jaws even when the men could hardly walk." So spoke Coleman, the gallant American volunteer.

Up to now nothing had been seen of the French infantry, and the exposed British force had been hustled and harried by Von Kluck's great army without receiving any substantial support. This was through no want of loyalty, but our gallant Allies were themselves hard pressed. Sir John French had sent urgent representations, especially to General Sordet, the leader of the cavalry operating upon the western side, and he had, as already shown, done what he could to screen Smith-Dorrien's flank. Now at last the retiring Army was coming in touch with those supports which were so badly needed. But before they were reached, on the morning of the 27th, the Germans had again driven in the rearguard of the First Corps.

During the retreat of the First Corps its rear and a cavalry right flank had been covered by the 5th Cavalry Brigade (Chetwode). On August 28 the corps was continuing its march towards La Fère and the cavalry found itself near Cerizy. At this point the pursuing German horsemen came into touch with it. At about five in the afternoon, three squadrons of the enemy advanced upon one squadron of the Scots Greys, which had the support of J Battery. Being fired at, the Germans dismounted and attempted to advance upon foot, but the fire was so heavy that they could make no progress and their led horses stampeded. They retired, still on foot, followed up by a squadron of the 12th Lancers on their flank. The remainder of the 12th Lancers, supported by the Greys, rode into the dismounted dragoons with sword and lance, killing or wounding nearly all of them. A section of guns had fired over the heads of the British cavalry during the advance into a supporting body of German cavalry, who retired, leaving many dead behind them. The whole hostile force retreated northwards, while the British cavalry continued to conform to the movements of the First Corps. In this spirited little action the German regiment engaged was, by the irony of fate, the 1st Guard Dragoons, Queen Victoria's Own. The British lost 43 killed and wounded. Among the dead were Major Swetenham and Captain Michell of the 12th Lancers. Colonel Wormald of the same regiment was wounded. The excited troopers rode back triumphantly between the guns of J Battery, the cavalrymen exchanging cheers with the horse-gunners as they passed, and brandishing their blood-stained weapons.

On the evening before this brisk skirmish, the flank-guards of the British saw a considerable body of troops in dark clothing upon their left, and shortly afterwards perceived the shell-bursts of a rapid and effective fire over the pursuing German batteries. It was the first contact with the advancing French. These men consisted of the Sixty-first and Sixty-second French Reserve Divisions, and were the van of a considerable army under General D'Amade. From that moment the British forces were at last enabled, after a week of constant marching, covering sometimes a good thirty miles a day, and four days of continual fighting against extreme odds, to feel that they had reached a zone of comparative quiet.

The German cavalry still followed the Army upon its southerly march, but there was no longer any fear of a disaster, for the main body of the Army was unbroken, and the soldiers were rather exasperated than depressed by their experience. On the Friday and Saturday, however,

August 28 and 29, considerable crowds of stragglers and fugitives, weary and often weaponless, appeared upon the lines of communication, causing the utmost consternation by their stories and their appearance. Few who endured the mental anxiety caused in Great Britain by the messages of Sunday, August 30, are likely to forget it. The reports gave an enormous stimulus to recruiting, and it is worthy of record and remembrance that, in the dark week which followed before the true situation was clearly discerned, every successive day brought as many recruits to the standards as are usually gained in a year. Such was the rush of men that the authorities, with their many preoccupations, found it very difficult to deal with them. A considerable amount of hardship and discomfort was the result, which was endured with good humour until it could be remedied. It is to be noted in this connection that it was want of arms which held back the new armies. He who compares the empty arsenals of Britain with the huge extensions of Krupp's, undertaken during the years before the war, will find the final proof as to which Power deliberately planned it.

To return to the fortunes of the men retreating from Le Cateau, the colonels and brigadiers had managed to make order out of what was approaching to chaos on the day that the troops left St. Quentin. The feet of many were so cut and bleeding that they could no longer limp along, so some were packed into a few trains available and others were hoisted on to limbers, guns, wagons, or anything with wheels, some carts being lightened of ammunition or stores to make room for helpless men. In many cases the whole kits of the officers were deliberately sacrificed. Many men were delirious from exhaustion and incapable of understanding an order. By the evening of the 27th the main body of the troops were already fifteen miles south of the Somme river and canal, on the line Nesle–Ham–Flavy. All day there was distant shelling from the pursuers, who sent their artillery freely forward with their cavalry.

On August 30, the whole Army having crossed the Oise, the bridges over that river were destroyed, an operation which was performed under a heavy shell fire, and cost the lives of several sapper officers and men. No words can exaggerate what the Army owed to Wilson's sappers of the 56th and 57th Field Companies and 3rd Signal Company, as also to Tulloch's, of the 17th and 59th Companies and 5th Signal Company, whose work was incessant, fearless, and splendid.

The Army continued to fall back on the line of the Aisne, the general direction being almost east and west through Crépy-en-Valois. The aeroplanes, which had conducted a fine service during the whole of the operations, reported that the enemy was still coming rapidly on, and streaming southwards in the Compiègne direction. That they were in touch was shown in dramatic fashion upon the early morning of September 1. The epic in question deserves to be told somewhat fully, as being one of those incidents which are mere details in the history of a campaign, and yet may live as permanent inspirations in the life of an army.

The 1st Cavalry Brigade, greatly exhausted after screening the retreat so long, was encamped near Néry, to the south of Compiègne, the bivouac being a somewhat extended one. Two units were close to each other and to the brigade headquarters of General Briggs. These were the hard-worked 2nd Dragoon Guards (the Bays) and L Battery of Horse Artillery. Reveille was at four o'clock, and shortly after that hour both troopers and gunners were busy in leading their horses to water. It was a misty morning, and, peering through the haze, an officer perceived that from the top of a low hill about seven hundred yards away three mounted men were looking down upon them. They were the observation officers of three four-gun German batteries. Before the British could realise the situation the guns dashed up and came into action with shrapnel at point-blank range. The whole twelve poured their fire into the disordered bivouac before them. The slaughter and confusion were horrible. Numbers of the horses and men were killed or wounded, and three of the guns were dismounted. It was a most complete surprise, and promised to be an absolute disaster. A body of German cavalry had escorted the guns, and their rifles added to the volume of fire.

It is at such moments that the grand power of disciplined valour comes to bring order out of chaos. Everything combined to make defence difficult – the chilling hour of the morning, the suddenness of the attack,

Typical scenes from a British encampment.

its appalling severity, and the immediate loss of guns and men. A sunken road ran behind the British position, and from the edge of this the dismounted cavalrymen brought their rifles and their machine-gun into action. They suffered heavily from the pelting gusts of shrapnel. Young Captain de Crespigny, the gallant cadet of a gallant family, and many other good men were beaten down by it. The sole hope lay in the guns. Three were utterly disabled. There was a rush of officers and men to bring the other three into action. Sclater-Booth, the major of the battery, and one lieutenant were already down. Captain Bradbury took command and cheered on the men. Two of the guns were at once put out of action, so all united to work the one that remained.

What followed was Homeric. Lieutenant Giffard in rushing forward was hit in four places. Bradbury's leg was shattered, but he lay beside the trail encouraging the others and giving his directions. Lieutenant Mundy, standing wide as observation officer, was mortally wounded. The limber could not be got alongside and the shell had to be man-handled.

In bringing it up Lieutenant Campbell was shot. Immediately afterwards another shell burst over the gun, killed the heroic Bradbury, and wounded Sergeant Dorell, Driver Osborne, and Gunners Nelson and Derbyshire, the only remaining men. But the fight went on. The bleeding men served the gun so long as they could move, Osborne and Derbyshire crawling over with the shells while Nelson loaded and Dorell laid. Osborne and Derbyshire fainted from loss of blood and lay between limber and gun. But the fight went on. Dorell and Nelson, wounded and exhausted, crouched behind the shield of the thirteen-pounder and kept up an incessant fire. Now it was that the amazing fact became visible that all this devotion had not been in vain. The cluster of Bays on the edge of the sunken road burst out into a cheer, which was taken up by the staff, who, with General Briggs himself, had come into the firing-line. Several of the German pieces had gone out of action. The dying gun had wrought good work, as had the Maxim of the Bays in the hands of Lieutenant Lamb. Some at least of its opponents had been silenced before the two brave gunners could do no more, for their strength had gone with their blood. Not only had the situation been saved, but victory had been assured.

About eight in the morning news of the perilous situation had reached the 19th Brigade. The 1st Middlesex, under Colonel Rowley, was hurried forward, followed by the 1st Scottish Rifles. Marching rapidly upon the firing, after the good old Maxim, the Middlesex found themselves in a position to command the German batteries. After two minutes of rapid fire it was seen that the enemy had left their guns. Eight guns were captured, two of them still loaded. About a dozen German gunners lay dead or wounded round them. Twenty-five of the escort were captured, as was an ambulance with some further prisoners a mile in the rear. The cavalry, notably the 11th Hussars, endeavoured to follow up the success, but soon found themselves in the presence of superior forces. New wheels and new wheelers were found for the injured guns, and Battery L came intact out of action – intact save for the brave acolytes who should serve her no more. Bradbury, Nelson, and Doxell had the Victoria Cross, and never was it better earned. The battery itself was recalled to England to refit and the guns were changed for new ones. It is safe to say that for many a long year these shrapnel-dinted thirteen-pounders will serve as a monument of one of those deeds which, by their self-sacrifice and nobility, do something to mitigate the squalors and horrors of war.

The German advance guards were particularly active upon this day, September 1, the anniversary of Sedan. Although the Soissons Bridge had been destroyed they had possession of another at Vic, and over this they poured in pursuit of the First Corps, overtaking about 8 A.M. near Villars-Cotteret the rearguard, consisting of the Irish Guards and the 2nd Coldstream. The whole of the 4th Guards Brigade was drawn into the fight, which resolved itself into a huge rifle duel amid thick woods, Scott-Kerr, their Brigadier, riding up and down the firing line. The Guards retired slowly upon the 6th Infantry Brigade (Davies), which was aided by Lushington's 41st Brigade of Artillery, just south of Pisseleux. The Germans had brought up many guns, but could make no further progress, and the British position was held until 6 P.M., when the rearguard closed up with the rest of the Army. Lushington's guns had fought with no infantry in front of them, and it was a matter of great difficulty in the end to get them off, but it was accomplished by some very brilliant work under an infernal fire. After this sharp action, in which Colonel Morris of the Irish Guards lost his life, the retreat of the First Army Corps was not seriously interfered with. The losses at that date in this corps amounted to 81 officers and 2180 of all ranks.

On the night of September 1, the First and Second Army Corps were in touch once more at Betz, and were on the move again by 2 A.M. upon the 2nd. On this morning the German advance was curiously interlocked with the British rear, and four German guns were picked up by the cavalry near Ermenonville. They are supposed to have been the remaining guns of the force which attacked Battery L at Néry. The movements of the troops during the day were much impeded by the French refugees, who thronged every road in their flight before the German terror. In spite of these obstructions, the rearward services of the Army – Supply columns, ammunition columns, and medical transport – were well conducted,

A destroyed bridge at Soissons.

and the admiration of all independent observers. The work of all these departments had been greatly complicated by the fact that, as the Channel ports were now practically undefended and German troops, making towards the coast, had cut the main Calais-Boulogne line at Amiens, the base had been moved farther south from Havre to St. Nazaire, which meant shifting seventy thousand tons of stores and changing all arrangements. In spite of this the supplies were admirable. It may safely be said that if there is one officer more than another for whom the whole British Army felt a glow of gratitude, it was for Sir William Robertson, the Chief of the Commissariat, who saw that the fighting man was never without his rations. Greatly also did they appreciate the work of his subordinates, who, wet or fine, through rainfall or shell-fall, passed the food forward to the weary men at the front.

A difficult movement lay in front of the Army which had to cross the Marne, involving a flank march in the face of the enemy. A retirement was still part of the general French scheme of defence, and the British Army had to conform to it, though it was exultantly whispered from officer to sergeant and from sergeant to private that the turn of the tide was nearly due. On this day it was first observed that the Germans, instead of pushing forward, were swinging across to the east in the direction of Château-Thierry. This made the task of the British a more easy one, and before evening they were south of the Marne and had blown up the bridges. The movement of the Germans brought them down to the river, but at a point some ten miles east of the British position. They were reported to be crossing the river at La Ferté, and Sir John French continued to fall back towards the Seine, moving after sundown, as the heat had been for some days very exhausting. The troops halted in the neighbourhood of Presles, and were cheered by the arrival of some small drafts, numbering about 2000, a first installment towards refilling the great gaps in the ranks, which at this date could not have been less than from 12,000 to 15,000 officers and men.

Here for a moment this narrative may be broken, since it has taken the Army to the farthest point of its retreat and reached that moment of advance for which every officer and man, from Sir John French to the drummer-boys, was eagerly waiting. With their left flank resting upon the extreme outer forts of Paris, the British troops had finally ended a retreat which will surely live in military history as a remarkable example of an army retaining its cohesion and courage in the presence of an overpowering adversary, who could never either cut them off or break in their rearguard. The British Army was a small force when compared with the giants of the Continent, but when tried by this supreme test it is not mere national complacency for us to claim that it lived up to its own highest traditions. "It was not to forts of steel and concrete that the Allies owed their strength," said a German historian, writing of this phase of the war, "but to the magnificent qualities of the British Army." We desire no compliments at the expense of our brothers-in-arms, nor would they be just, but at least so generous a sentence as this may be taken as an advance from that contemptuous view of the British Army with which the campaign had begun.

The Battle of the Aisne

THE stretch of river which confronted the British Army when they set about the hazardous crossing of Aisne was about fifteen miles in length. It lay as nearly as possible east and west, so that the advance was from south to north. As the British faced the hazardous river the First Army Corps was on the right of their line, together with half the cavalry. In the centre was the Second Corps, on the left the Third Corps, which was still without one of its divisions (the Sixth), but retained, on the other hand, the 19th Brigade, which did not belong to it. Each of these British corps covered a front of, roughly, five miles. Across the broad and swift river a considerable German army with a powerful artillery was waiting to dispute the passage. On the right of the British were the French Fifth and Seventh Armies, and on their left, forming the extremity of the Allied line, was the French Sixth Army, acting in such close co-operation with the British Third Corps in the Soissons region that their guns were often turned upon the same point. This Sixth French Army, with the British Army, may be looked upon as the left wing of the huge Allied line which stretched away with many a curve and bend to the Swiss frontier. During all this hurried retreat from the Marne, it is to be remembered that the Eastern German armies had hardly moved at all. It was their four armies of the right which had swung back like a closing door, the Crown Prince's Fifth Army being the hinge upon which it turned. Now the door had ceased to swing, and one solid barrier presented itself to the Allies. It is probable that the German preponderance of numbers was, for the moment, much lessened or even had ceased to exist, for the losses in battle, the detachments for Russia, and the operations in Belgium had all combined to deplete the German ranks.

German trenches at the Aisne.

The Belgian Army had retired into Antwerp before the fall of Brussels, but they were by no means a force to be disregarded, being fired by that sense of intolerable wrong which is the most formidable stimulant to a virile nation. From the shelter of the Antwerp entrenchments they continually buzzed out against the German lines of communication, and although they were usually beaten back, and were finally pent in, they still added to the great debt of gratitude which the Allies already owed them by holding up a considerable body, two army corps at least, of good troops. On the other hand, the fortress of Maubeuge, on the northern French frontier, which had been invested within a few days of the battle of Mons, had now fallen before the heavy German guns, with the result that at least a corps of troops under Von Zwehl and these same masterful guns were now released for service on the Aisne.

The more one considers the operation of the crossing of the Aisne with the battle which followed it, the more one is impressed by the extraordinary difficulty of the task, the swift debonair way in which it was tackled, and the pushful audacity of the various commanders in gaining a foothold upon the farther side. Consider that upon the 12th the Army was faced by a deep, broad, unfordable river with only one practicable bridge in the fifteen miles opposite them. They had a formidable enemy armed with powerful artillery standing on the defensive upon a line of uplands commanding every crossing and approach, whilst the valley was so broad that ordinary guns upon the corresponding uplands could have no effect, and good positions lower down were hard to find. There was the problem. And yet upon the 14th the bulk of the Army was across and had established itself in positions from which it could never afterwards be driven. All arms must have worked well to bring about such a result, but what can be said of the Royal Engineers, who built under heavy fire in that brief space nine bridges, some of them capable of taking heavy traffic, while they restored five of the bridges which the enemy had destroyed! September 13, 1914, should be recorded in their annals as a marvellous example of personal self-sacrifice and technical proficiency.

Sir John French, acting with great swiftness and decision, did not lose an hour after he had established himself in force upon the northern bank of the river in pushing his men ahead and finding out what was in front of him. The weather was still very wet, and heavy mists drew a veil over the German dispositions, but the advance went forward. The British right wing, consisting of the First Division of the Aisne. First Corps, had established itself most securely, as was natural, since it was the one corps which had formed an unbroken bridge in front of it. The First Division had pushed forward as far as Moulins and Vendresse, which lie about two miles north of the river. Now, in the early hours of the 14th, the whole of the Second Division got over. The immediate narrative, therefore, is concerned with the doings of the two divisions of the First Corps, upon which fell the first and chief strain of the very important and dangerous advance upon that date.

On the top of the line of chalk hills which faced the British was an ancient and famous highway, the Chemin-des-Dames, which, like all ancient highways, had been carried along the crest of the ridge. This was in the German possession, and it became the objective of the British attack. The 2nd Infantry Brigade (Bulfin's) led the way, working upwards in the early morning from Moulins and Vendresse through the hamlet of Troyon towards the great road. This brigade, consisting of the 2nd Sussex, 1st Northamptons, 1st North Lancashire, and 2nd Rifles, drawn mostly from solid shire regiments, was second to none in the Army. Just north of Troyon was a considerable deserted sugar factory, which formed a feature in the landscape. It lay within a few hundred yards of the Chemin-des-Dames, while another winding road, cut in the side of the hill, lay an equal distance to the south of it, and was crossed by the British in their advance. This road, which was somewhat sunken in the chalk, and thus offered some cover to a crouching man, played an important part in the operations.

Lieutenant Balfour and a picket of the 2nd Rifles, having crept up and reconnoitred the factory, returned with the information that it was held by the Germans, and that twelve guns were in position three hundred yards to the east of it. General Bulfin then – it was about 3:30 in the morning of a wet, misty day – sent the 2nd Rifles, the 2nd Sussex Regiment, and the 1st NorthamptonS forward, with the factory and an adjoining whitewashed farmhouse as their objective. The 1st North Lancashires remained in reserve at Vendresse. The attacking force was under the immediate command of Colonel Serocold of the Rifles. The three advanced regiments drove in the pickets of the Germans, and after a severe fight turned the enemy out of his front trench, A Company of the Sussex capturing several hundred prisoners. A number of men, however, including Colonel Montresor and Major Cookson, were shot while rounding up these Germans and sending them to the rear. The advanced line had suffered severely, so the North Lancashires were called up and launched at the sugar factory, which they carried with a magnificent bayonet attack in spite of a fierce German resistance. Their losses were very heavy, including Major Lloyd, their commander, but their victory was a glorious one. The two batteries of the enemy were now commanded by machine-guns, brought up to the factory by Lieutenant Dashwood of the Sussex. The enemy made a brave attempt to get these guns away, but the teams and men were shot down, and it was a German Colenso. The British, however, unlike the Boers, were unable to get away the prizes of their victory. The factory was abandoned as it was exposed to heavy fire, and the four regiments formed a firing-line, taking such cover as they could find, but a German shell fire developed which was so deadly that they were unable to get forward.

A small party of Rifles, under Cathcart and Foljambe, clung hard to the captured guns, sending repeated messages: "For God's sake bring horses and fetch away these pieces!" No horses were, however, available, and eventually both the guns and the buildings were regained by the Germans, the former being disabled before they were abandoned by their captors, and the factory being smashed by the shells. Major Green and a company of the Sussex, with some of the Coldstream under Major Grant, had got as far forward as the Chemin-des-Dames, but fell back steadily when their flank was finally exposed. Two companies of the 1st Coldstream, under Colonel Ponsonby, had also pushed on to the road, and now came back. Nothing could exceed the desperate gallantry of officers and men. Major Jelf, severely wounded, cheered on his riflemen until evening. Major Warre of the same regiment and Major Phillips rallied the hard-pressed line again and again. Lieutenant Spread, of the Lancashires, worked his machine-gun until it was smashed, and then, wounded as he was, brought up a second gun and continued the fight. Major Burrows rallied the Lancashires when their leader, Major Lloyd, was hit. Brigade-Major Watson, of the Queen's, was everywhere in the thick of the firing. No men could have been better led, nor could any leaders have better men. A large number of wounded, both British and Germans, lay under the shelter of some haystacks between the lines, and crawled slowly round them for shelter, as the fire came from one side or the other – a fitting subject surely for a Verestschagin!

Meanwhile, it is necessary to follow what had been going on at the immediate left of Bulfin's Brigade. Maxse's 1st Brigade had moved up in the face of a considerable fire until it came to be nearly as far north as the factory, but to the west of it. The 1st Coldstream had been sent across to help the dismounted cavalry to cover Bulfin's right, since the main German strength seemed to be in that quarter. The 1st Scots Guards was held in reserve, but the other regiments of the 1st Brigade, the 1st Black Watch and the 1st Camerons, a battalion which had taken the place of the brave but unfortunate Munsters, lined up on the left of the factory and found themselves swept by the same devastating fire which had checked the advance. This fire came from the fringe of the woods and from a line of trenches lying north-east of the factory on the edge of the Chemin-des-dames. Up to this time the British had no artillery support on account of the mist, but now Geddes' 25th Brigade R.F.A., comprising the 113th, 114th, and 115th Batteries, was brought to its assistance. It could do little good in such a dim light, and one battery, the 115th, under Major Johnstone, which pushed up within eight hundred yards of the enemy's position, was itself nearly destroyed. The 116th R.F.A., under Captain Oliver, also did great work, working its way up till it was almost in the infantry line, and at one time in advance of it. The whole infantry line, including a mixture of units, men of the Rifles, Sussex, and North Lancashires, with a sprinkling of Guardsmen and Black Watch from the 1st Brigade, came slowly down the hill – "sweating blood to hold their own," as one of them described it – until they reached the sunken road which has been already mentioned. There General Bulfin had stationed himself with the reserve, and the line steadied itself, re-formed, and, with the support of the guns, made head once more against the advancing Germans, who were unable to make any progress against the fire which was poured into them. With such spades and picks as could be got, a line of shallow trenches was thrown up, and these were held against all attacks for the rest of the day.

It was the haphazard line of these hurriedly dug shelters which determined the position retained in the weeks to come. As this was the apex of the British advance and all the corps upon the left were in turn brought to a standstill and driven to make trenches, the whole line of the First Corps formed a long diagonal slash across the hillside, with its right close to the Chemin-des-Dames and its left upon the river in the neighbourhood of Chavonne. The result was that now and always the trenches of the 2nd Brigade were in an extremely exposed position, for they were open not only to the direct fire of the Germans, which was not very severe, but to an enfilading fire from more distant guns upon each flank. Their immediate neighbours upon the right were the 1st Queen's Surrey, acting as flank-guard, and a Moroccan corps from the Fifth French chapter Army, which had not reached so advanced a position, but was in echelon upon their right rear.

It has already been shown how the 1st Brigade was divided up, the 1st Coldstream being on the right of the 2nd Brigade. The rest of the 1st Brigade had carried out an advance parallel to that described, and many of the Black Watch, who were the right-hand regiment, got mixed with Bulfin's men when they were driven back to what proved to be the permanent British line. This advance of the 1st Brigade intercepted a strong force of the enemy which was creeping round the left flank of the 2nd Brigade. The counter-stroke brought the flank attack to a standstill. The leading regiments of the 1st Brigade suffered very severely, however, especially the Cameron Highlanders, whose gallantry carried them far to the front. This regiment lost Lieutenant-Colonel MacLachlan, 2 majors, Maitland and Nicholson, 3 captains, 11 lieutenants, and about 300 rank and file in the action. Some of these fell into the hands of the enemy, but the great majority were killed or wounded. The 1st Scots Guards upon the left of the brigade had also heavy casualties, while the Black Watch lost their Colonel, Grant Duff, their Adjutant, Rowan Hamilton, and many men. When the line on their right fell back, they conformed to the movement until they received support from two companies of the 1st Gloucesters from the 3rd Brigade upon their left rear.

The 4th (Guards) Brigade, forming the left of the Second Division, was across the river in battle array by ten o'clock in the morning and moving northwards towards the village of Ostel. Its task was a supremely difficult one. Dense woods faced it, fringed with the hostile riflemen, while a heavy shell-fire tore through the extended ranks. It is safe to say that such an advance could not have been carried out in the heavy-handed German fashion without annihilating losses. As it was, the casualties were heavy, but not sufficient to prevent a continuance of the attack, which at one o'clock carried the farm and trenches which were its objective. The steep slopes and the thick woods made artillery support impossible, though one section of a battery did contrive to keep up with the infantry. The 3rd Coldstream being held up in their advance on the Soupir front, the 1st Irish were moved up on their right flank, but the line could do little more than hold its own. Captain Berners, Lord Guernsey, Lord Arthur Hay, and others were killed at this point. The German infantry advanced several times to counter-attack, but were swept back by the fire of the Guards.

At one period it was found that the general German advance, which had followed the holding of the British attack, was threatening to flow in between the two divisions of the First Army Corps. The 3rd Brigade (Landon's) was therefore deployed rapidly from the point about a mile south of Vernesse where it had been stationed. Two regiments of the brigade, the 2nd Welsh and the 1st South Wales Borderers, were flung against the heavy German column advancing down the Beaulne ridge and threatening to cut Haig's corps in two. The Welshmen, worthy successors of their ancestors who left such a name on the battlefields of France, succeeded in heading it off and driving it back so that they were able to extend and get in touch with the right of the Second Division. This consisted of the 5th Brigade (Haking's) with the 6th (Davies') upon its left. Both of these brigades had to bear the brunt of continual German counter-attacks, involving considerable losses, both from shell and rifle fire. In spite of this they won their way for a mile or more up the slopes, where they were brought to a standstill and dug themselves into temporary shelter, continuing the irregular diagonal line of trenches which had been started by the brigades upon the right.

It is impossible not to admire the way in which the German general in command observed and attempted to profit by any gap in the British line. It has already been shown how he tried to push his column between the two divisions of the First Corps and was only stopped by the deployment of the 3rd Brigade. Later, an even fairer chance presented itself, and he was quick to take advantage of it. The advance of the Guards Brigade to the Ostel ridge had caused a considerable gap between them and the nearest unit of the Second Corps, and also between the First Corps and the river. A German attack came swarming down upon the weak spot. From Troyon to Ostel, over five miles of ground, Haig's corps was engaged to the last man and pinned down in their positions. It was not possible to fill the gap. Not to fill it might have meant disaster – disaster under heavy shell-fire with an unfordable river in the rear. Here was a supreme example of the grand work that was done when our cavalry were made efficient as dismounted riflemen. Their mobility brought them quickly to the danger spot. Their training turned them in an instant from horsemen to infantry. The 15th Hussars, the Irish Horse, the whole of Briggs' 1st Cavalry Brigade, and finally the whole of De Lisle's 2nd Cavalry Brigade, were thrown into the gap. The German advance was stayed and the danger passed. From now onwards the echelon formed by the units of the First Corps ended with these cavalry brigades near Chavonne to the immediate north of the river.

The Third Division of the Second Corps, being on the immediate left of the operations which have been already described, moved forward upon Aizy, which is on about the same level as Ostel, the objective of the Guards. The 8th (Doran's) Brigade moved north by a tributary stream which runs down to the Aisne, while the 9th (Shaw's) tried to advance in line with it on the plateau to the right. Both brigades found it impossible to get any farther, and established themselves in entrenchments about a mile north of Vailly, so as to cover the important bridge at that place, where the 7th Brigade was in reserve. The three Fusilier regiments of the 9th Brigade all lost heavily, and the Lincolns had at one time to recross the river, but recovered their position.

The attack made by the Fifth Division near Missy was held up by a very strong German position among the woods on the Chivres heights which was fronted by wire entanglements. The regiments chiefly engaged were the Norfolks and Bedfords of the 15th Brigade, with the Cornwalls and East Surreys of the 14th Brigade, the remains of the Cheshires being in close support. They crossed the wire and made good progress at first, but were eventually brought to a stand by heavy fire at close range from a trench upon their right front. It was already dusk, so the troops ended by maintaining the position at Missy and Ste. Marguerite, where there were bridges to be guarded.

The Fourth Division of Pulteney's Third Corps had no better success, and was only able to maintain its ground. It may be remarked, as an example of valiant individual effort, that this division was largely indebted for its ammunition supply to the efforts of Captain Johnston of the Sappers, who, upon a crazy raft of his own construction, aided by Lieutenant Flint, spent twelve hours under fire ferrying over the precious boxes. The familiar tale of stalemate was to be told of the Sixth French Army in the Soissons section of the river. Along the whole Allied line the position was the same, the greatest success and probably the hardest fighting having fallen to the lot of the Eighteenth French Corps, which had taken, lost, and finally retaken Craonne, thus establishing itself upon the lip of that formidable plateau which had been the objective of all the attacks.

In the Vailly region the 5th Cavalry Brigade found itself in a difficult position, for it had crossed the stream as a mounted unit in expectation of a pursuit, and now found itself under heavy fire in the village of Vailly with no possibility of getting forward. The only alternative was to recross the river by the single narrow bridge, which was done at a later date under very heavy fire, the troopers leading their horses over in single file. This difficult operation was superintended by Captain Wright of the Engineers, the same brave officer who had endeavoured to blow up the bridge at Mons. Unhappily, he was mortally wounded on this occasion. On the afternoon of the 14th – it being found that the British artillery was shelling our own advanced trenches – Staff-Captain Harter of the 9th Brigade galloped across the bridge and informed the gunners as to the true position.

Towards evening, in spite of the fact that there were no reserves and that all the troops had endured heavy losses and great fatigue, a general advance was ordered in the hope of gaining the high ground of the

Chemin-des-Dames before night. It was nearly sunset when the orders were given, and the troops responded gallantly to the call, though many of them had been in action since daybreak. The fire, however, was very heavy, and no great progress could be made. The First Division gained some ground, but was brought to a standstill. The only brigade which made good headway was Haking's 5th, which reached the crest of the hill in the neighbourhood of Tilleul-de-Courtecon. General Haking sent out scouts, and finding German outposts upon both his flanks, he withdrew under cover of darkness.

Thus ended the sharp and indecisive action of September 14, the Germans holding their ground, but being in turn unable to drive back the Allies, who maintained their position and opposed an impassable obstacle to the renewed advance upon Paris. The battle was marked by the common features of advance, arrest, and entrenchment, which occurred not only in the British front, but in that of the French armies upon either flank. When the action ceased, the 1st Northamptons and the 1st Queen's, sent to guard the pressure point at the extreme right of the line, had actually reached the Chemin-des-Dames, the British objective, and had dug themselves in upon the edge of it. From this very advanced spot the British line extended diagonally across the hillside for many miles until it reached the river. Several hundred prisoners and some guns were taken in the course of the fighting. When one considers the predominant position of the Germans, and that their artillery was able to give them constant assistance, whereas that of the British and French was only brought up with the utmost difficulty, we can only marvel that the infantry were able to win and to hold the ground.

The next day, September 15, was spent for the most part in making good the position gained and deepening the trenches to get some protection from the ever-growing artillery fire, which was the more intense as the great siege guns from Maubeuge were upon this day, for the first time, brought into action. At first the terrific explosions of these shells, the largest by far which had ever been brought into an actual line of battle, were exceedingly alarming, but after a time it became realised that, however omnipotent they might be against iron or concrete, they were comparatively harmless in soft soil, where their enormous excavations were soon used as convenient ready-made rifle-pits by the soldiers. This heavy fire led to a deepening of the trenches, which necessitated a general levy of picks and shovels from the country round, for a large portion of such equipment had been lost in the first week of the campaign.

Only two active movements were made in the course of the day, one being that Hamilton's Third Division advanced once more towards Aizy and established itself a mile or more to the north in a better tactical position. The 7th Brigade suffered considerable casualties in this change, including Colonel Hasted, of the 1st Wilts. The other was that Ferguson's Fifth Division fell back from Chivres, where it was exposed to a cross fire, and made its lines along the river bank, whence the Germans were never able to drive it, although they were only four hundred yards away in a position which was high above it. For the rest, it was a day of navvy's toil, though the men worked alternately with rifle and with pick, for there were continual German advances which withered away before the volleys which greeted them. By the 16th the position was fairly secure, and on the same day a welcome reinforcement arrived in the shape of the Sixth Division, forming the missing half of Pulteney's Third Corps.

This division was kept in reserve upon the south side of the river. The French Commander-in-Chief had intimated that he intended to throw in reinforcements upon the left of the Sixth French Army, and so, as he hoped, to turn the German right. It was determined, therefore, that there should be no attempt at a British advance, but that the Allies should be content with holding the enemy to his positions. The two armies lay facing each other, therefore, at an average distance of about five hundred yards. The pressure was still most severe upon the 2nd Brigade on the extreme right. Bulfin's orders were to hold on at all costs, as he was the pivot of the whole line. He and his men responded nobly to the responsibility, although both they and their neighbours of Maxse's 1st Brigade had sustained a loss of over 1000 men each upon the 14th – 25 per cent of their number. The shell-fire was incessant and from several converging directions. German infantry attacks were constant by night and by day, and the undrained trenches were deep in water. The men lay without overcoats and drenched to the skin, for the rain was incessant. Yet the sixth day found them on the exact ground upon which they had thrown their weary bodies after their attack. Nations desire from time to time to be reassured as to their own virility. Neither in endurance nor in courage have the British departed from the traditions of their ancestors. The unending strain of the trenches reached the limits of human resistance. But the line was always held.

On September 16 occurred an incident which may be taken as typical of the difference in the spirit with which the British and the Germans make war. Close to the lines of the Guards a barn which contained fifty wounded Germans was ignited by the enemy's shells. Under a terrific fire a rescue party rushed forward and got the unfortunate men to a place of safety.

Several of the British lost their lives in this exploit, including Dr. Huggan, the Scottish International footballer. The Germans mock at our respect for sport, and yet this is the type of man that sport breeds, and it

Stretcher bearers struggle through a sea of mud.

is the want of them in their own ranks which will stand for ever between us.

September 17 was a day of incessant attacks upon the right of the line, continually repulsed and yet continually renewed. One can well sympathise with the feelings of the German commanders who, looking down from their heights, saw the British line in a most dangerous strategical position, overmatched by their artillery, with a deep river in their rear, and yet were unable to take advantage of it because of their failure to carry the one shallow line of extemporised trenches. Naturally, they came again and again, by night and by day, with admirable perseverance and daring to the attack, but were always forced to admit that nothing can be done against the magazine rifle in hands which know how to use it. They tried here and they tried there, these constant sudden outpourings of cheering, hurrying, grey-clad men. They were natural tactics, but expensive ones, for every new attack left a fresh fringe of stricken men in front of the British lines.

One incident upon the 17th stands out amid the somewhat monotonous record of trench attacks. On the extreme right of the British line a company of the 1st Northamptons occupied a most exposed position on the edge of the Chemin-des-Dames. The men in a German trench which was some hundreds of yards in front hoisted a white flag and then advanced upon the British lines. It is well to be charitable in all these white flag incidents, since it is always possible on either side that unauthorised men may hoist it and the officer in command very properly refuse to recognise it; but in this case the deception appears to have been a deliberate one. These are the facts. On seeing the flag, Captain Savage, of B Company Northamptons, got out of the trench and with Lieutenant Dimmer, of the Rifles, advanced to the Germans. He threw down his sword and revolver to show that he was unarmed. He found a difficulty in getting a direct answer from the Germans, so he saluted their officer, who returned his salute, and turned back to walk to his own trench. Dimmer, looking back, saw the Germans level their rifles, so he threw himself down, crying out, "For God's sake get down." Captain Savage stood erect and was riddled with bullets. Many of

81

the Northamptons, including Lieutenant Gordon, were shot down by the same volley. The Germans then attempted an advance, which was stopped by the machine-guns of the 1st Queen's. Such deplorable actions must always destroy all the amenities of civilised warfare. On the afternoon of the same day, September 17, a more serious attack was made upon the right flank of the advanced British position, the enemy reoccupying a line of trenches from which they had previously been driven. It was a dismal day of wind, rain, and mist, but the latter was not wholly an evil, as it enabled that hard-worked regiment, the 1st Northamptons, under their Colonel, Osborne Smith, to move swiftly forward and, with the help of the 1st Queen's, carry the place at the bayonet point. Half the Germans in the trench were put out of action, thirty-eight taken, and the rest fled. Pushing on after their success, they found the ridge beyond held by a considerable force of German infantry. The 2nd Rifles had come into the fight, and a dismounted squadron of the composite cavalry regiment put in some good work upon the flank. The action was continued briskly until dark, when both sides retained their ground with the exception of the captured line of trenches, which remained with the British. Seven officers and about 200 men were killed or wounded in this little affair.

The 18th found the enemy still acting upon the Napoleonic advice of *Tâtez toujours*. All day they were feeling for that weak place which could never be found. The constant attempts were carried on into the night with the same monotonous record of advance leading to repulse. At one time it was the line of the 1st Queen's – and no line in the Army would be less likely to give results. Then it was the left flank of the First Division, and then the front of the Second. Now and again there were swift counters from the British, in one of which an enemy's trench was taken by the 1st Gloucesters with the two machine-guns therein. But there was no inducement for any general British advance. "We have nothing to lose by staying here," said a General, "whereas every day is of importance to the Germans, so the longer we can detain them here the better." So it seemed from the point of view of the Allies. There is a German point of view also, however, which is worthy of consideration. They were aware, and others were not, that great reserves of men were left in the Fatherland, even as there were in France and in Britain, but that, unlike France and Britain, they actually had the arms and equipment for them, so that a second host could rapidly be called into the field. If these legions were in Belgium, they could ensure the fall of Antwerp, overrun the country, and seize the seaboard. All this could be effected while the Allies were held at the Aisne. Later, with these vast reinforcements, the German armies might burst the barrier which held them and make a second descent upon Paris, which was still only fifty miles away. So the Germans may have argued, and the history of the future was to show that there were some grounds for such a calculation. It was in truth a second war in which once again the Germans had the men and material ready, while the Allies had not.

This date, September 18, may be taken as the conclusion of the actual Battle of the Aisne, since from that time the operations defined themselves definitely as a mutual siege and gigantic artillery duel. The casualties of the British at the Aisne amounted, up to that date, to 10,000 officers and men, the great majority of which were suffered by Haig's First Army Corps. The action had lasted from the 13th, and its outstanding features, so far as our forces were concerned, may be said to have been the remarkable feat of crossing the river and the fine leadership of General Haig in the dangerous position in which he found himself. It has been suggested that the single unbroken bridge by which he crossed may have been a trap purposely laid by the Germans, whose plans miscarried owing to the simultaneous forcing of the river at many other points. As it was, the position of the First Corps was a very difficult one, and a reverse might have become an absolute disaster. It was impossible for General French to avoid this risk, for since the weather precluded all air reconnaissance, it was only by pushing his Army across that he could be sure of the enemy's dispositions. The net result was one more demonstration upon both sides that the defensive force has so great an advantage under modern conditions that if there be moderate equality of numbers, and if the flanks of each be guarded, a condition of stalemate will invariably ensue, until the campaign is decided by economic causes or by military movements in some other part of the field of operations.

There is ample evidence that for the time the German Army, though able with no great effort to hold the extraordinarily strong position which had been prepared for it, was actually in very bad condition. Large new drafts had been brought out, which had not yet been assimilated by the army. The resistance of Maubeuge had blocked one of their supply railroads, and for some time the commissariat had partially broken down. Above all, they were mentally depressed by meeting such resistance where they had been led to expect an easy victory, by their forced retreat when almost within sight of Paris, and by their losses, which had been enormous. In spite of their own great superiority in heavy guns, the French light field-pieces had controlled the battlefields. There is ample evidence in the letters which have been intercepted, apart from the statements and appearance of the prisoners, to show the want and depression which prevailed. This period, however, may be said to mark the nadir of the German fortunes in this year. The fall of Maubeuge improved their supplies of every sort, their reserves and Landwehr got broken in by the war of the trenches, and the eventual fall of Antwerp and invasion of Western Belgium gave them that moral stimulus which they badly needed.

It was at this time, September 20, that the Germans put a climax upon the long series of outrages and vandalisms of which their troops had been guilty by the bombardment of Rheims Cathedral, the Westminster Abbey of France. The act seems to have sprung from deliberate malice, for though it was asserted afterwards that the tower had been used as an artillery observation point, this is in the highest degree improbable, since the summit of the ridge upon the French side is available for such a purpose. The cathedral was occupied at the time by a number of German wounded, who were the sufferers by the barbarity of their fellow-countrymen. The incident will always remain as a permanent record of the value of that *Kultur* over which we have heard such frantic boasts. The records of the French, Belgian, and British Commissions upon the German atrocities, reinforced by the recollection of the burned University of Louvain and the shattered Cathedral of Rheims, will leave a stain upon the German armies which can never be erased. Their conduct is the more remarkable, since the invasion of 1870 was conducted with a stem but rigid discipline, which won the acknowledgment of the world. In spite of all the material progress and the superficial show of refinement, little more than a generation seems to have separated civilisation from primitive barbarity, which attained such a pitch that no arrangement could be made by which the wounded between the lines could be brought in. Such was the code of a nominally Christian nation in the year 1914.

Up to now the heavier end of the fighting had been borne by Haig's First Corps, but from the 20th onwards the Second and Third sustained the impact. The action just described, in which the West Yorkshires suffered so severely, was fought mainly by the 18th Brigade of Pulteney's Third Corps. On the 21st it was the turn of the Second Corps. During the night the 1st Wiltshire battalion of McCracken's 7th Brigade was attacked, and making a strong counter-attack in the morning they cleared a wood with the bayonet, and advanced the British line at that point. A subsequent

The ruin of the cathedral at Rheims.

attack upon the same brigade was repulsed. How heavy the losses had been in the wear and tear of six days' continual trench work is shown by the fact that when on this date the 9th Brigade (Shaw's) was taken back for a rest it had lost 30 officers and 860 men since crossing the Aisne.

The German heavy guns upon the 21st set fire to the village of Missy, but failed to dislodge the 1st East Surreys who held it. This battalion, in common with the rest of Ferguson's Division, were dominated night and day by a plunging fire from above. It is worth recording that in spite of the strain, the hardship, and the wet trenches, the percentage of serious sickness among the troops was lower than the normal rate of a garrison town. A few cases of enteric appeared about this time, of which six were in one company of the Coldstream Guards. It is instructive to note that in each case the man belonged to the uninoculated minority.

The attacks upon the British trenches, which had died down for several days, were renewed with considerable vigour upon September 26. The first, directed against the 1st Queen's, was carried out by a force of about 1000 men, who advanced in close order, and, coming under machine-gun fire, were rapidly broken up. The second was made by a German battalion debouching from the woods in front of the 1st South Wales Borderers. This attack penetrated the line at one point, the left company of the regiment suffering severely, with all its officers down. The reserve company, with the help of the 2nd Welsh Regiment, retook the trenches after a hot fight, which ended by the wood being cleared. The Germans lost heavily in this struggle, 80 of them being picked up on the very edge of the trench. The Borderers also had numerous casualties, which totalled up to 7 officers and 182 men, half of whom were actually killed.

The Army was now in a very strong position, for the trenches were so well constructed that unless a shell by some miracle went right in, no harm would result. The weather had become fine once more, and the flying service relieved the anxieties of the commanders as to a massed attack. The heavy artillery of the Allies was also improving from day to day, especially the heavy British howitzers, aided by aeroplane observers with a wireless installation. On the other hand, the guns were frequently hit by the enemy's fire. The 22nd R.F.A. lost a gun, the 50th three guns, and other batteries had similar losses. Concealment had not yet been reduced to a science.

At this period the enemy seems to have realised that his attacks, whether against the British line or against the French armies which flanked it, and had fought throughout with equal tenacity, were a mere waste of life. The assaults died away or became mere demonstrations. Early in October the total losses of the Army upon the Aisne had been 561 officers and 12,980 men, a proportion which speaks well for the coolness and accuracy of the enemy's sharp-shooters, while it exhibits our own forgetfulness of the lessons of the African War, where we learned that the officer should be clad and armed so like the men as to be indistinguishable even at short ranges. Of this large total the Second Corps lost 136 officers and 3095 men, and the First Corps 348 officers and 6073 men, the remaining 77 officers and 3812 men being from the Third Corps and the cavalry.

It was at this period that a great change came over both the object and the locality of the operations. This change depended upon two events which had occurred far to the north, and reacted upon the great armies locked in the long grapple of the Aisne. The first of these controlling circumstances was that, by the movement of the old troops and the addition of new ones, each army had sought to turn the flank of the other in the north, until the whole centre of gravity of the war was transferred to that region. A new French army under General Castelnau, whose fine defence of Nancy had put him in the front of French leaders, had appeared on the extreme left wing of the Allies, only to be countered by fresh bodies of Germans, until the ever-extending line lengthened out to the manufacturing districts of Lens and Lille, where amid pit-shafts and slag-heaps the cavalry of the French and the Germans tried desperately to get round each other's flank. The other factor was the fall of Antwerp, which had released very large bodies of Germans, who were flooding over Western Belgium, and, with the help of great new levies from Germany, carrying the war to the sand-dunes of the coast. The operations which brought about this great change open up a new chapter in the history of the war. The actual events which culminated in the fall of Antwerp may be very briefly handled, since, important as they were, they were not primarily part of the British task, and hence hardly come within the scope of this narrative.

The Belgians, after the evacuation of Brussels in August, had withdrawn their army into the widespread fortress of Antwerp, from which they made frequent sallies upon the Germans who were garrisoning their country. Great activity was shown and several small successes were gained, which had the useful effect of detaining two corps which might have been employed upon the Aisne. Eventually, towards the end of September, the Germans turned their attention seriously to the reduction of the city, with a well founded confidence that no modern forts could resist the impact of their enormous artillery. They drove the garrison within the lines, and early in October opened a bombardment upon the outer forts with such results that it was evidently only a matter of days before they would fall and the fine old city be faced with the alternative of surrender or destruction. The Spanish fury of Parma's pikemen would be a small thing compared to the *furor Teutonicus* working its evil deliberate will upon town-hall or cathedral, with the aid of fire-disc, petrol-spray, or other products of culture. The main problem before the Allies, if the town could not be saved, was to ensure that the Belgian army should be extricated and that nothing of military value which could be destroyed should be left to the invaders. No troops were available for a rescue, for the French and British old formations were already engaged, while the new ones were not yet ready for action. In these circumstances, a resolution was come to by the British leaders which was bold to the verge of rashness and so chivalrous as to be almost quixotic. It was determined to send out at the shortest notice a naval division, one brigade of which consisted of marines, troops who are second to none in the country's service, while the other two brigades were young amateur sailor volunteers, most of whom had only been under arms for a few weeks. It was an extraordinary experiment, as testing how far the average sport-loving, healthy-minded young Briton needs only his equipment to turn him into a soldier who, in spite of all rawness and inefficiency, can still affect the course of a campaign. This strange force, one-third veterans and two-thirds practically civilians, was hurried across to do what it could for the failing town, and to demonstrate to Belgium how real was the sympathy which prompted us to send all that we had. A reinforcement of a very different quality was dispatched a few days later in the shape of the Seventh Division of the Regular Army, with the Third Division of Cavalry. These fine troops were too late, however, to save the city, and soon found themselves in a position where it needed all their hardihood to save themselves.

The Marine Brigade of the Naval Division under General Paris was dispatched from England in the early morning and reached Antwerp during the night of October 3. They were about 2000 in number. Early next morning they were out in the trenches, relieving some weary Belgians. The Germans were already within the outer enceinte and drawing close to the inner. For forty-eight hours they held the line in the face of heavy shelling. The cover was good and the losses were not heavy. At the end of that time the Belgian troops, who had been a good deal worn by their heroic exertions, were unable to sustain the German pressure, and evacuated the trenches on the flank of the British line. The brigade then fell back to a reserve position in front of the town.

On the night of the 5th the two other brigades of the division, numbering some 5000 amateur sailors, arrived in Antwerp, and the whole force assembled on the new line of defence. Mr. Winston Churchill showed his gallantry as a man, and his indiscretion as a high official, whose life was of great value to his country by accompanying the force from England. The bombardment was now very heavy, and the town was on fire in several places. The equipment of the British left much to be desired, and their trenches were as indifferent as their training. None the less they played the man and lived up to the traditions of that great service upon whose threshold they stood. For three days these men, who a few weeks before had been anything from schoolmasters to tram-conductors, held their perilous post. They were very raw, but they possessed a great asset in their officers, who were usually men of long service. But neither the lads of the naval brigades nor the war-worn and much-enduring Belgians could stop the mouths of those inexorable guns. On the 8th it was clear that the forts could no longer be held. The British task had been to maintain the trenches which connected the forts with each other, but if the forts went it was clear that the trenches must be outflanked and untenable. The situation, therefore, was hopeless, and all that remained was to save the garrison and leave as little as possible for the victors. Some thirty or forty German merchant ships in the harbour were sunk and the great petrol tanks were set on fire. By the light of the flames the Belgian and British forces made their way successfully out of the town, and the good service rendered later by our Allies upon the Yser and elsewhere is the best justification of the policy which made us strain every nerve in order to do everything which could have a moral or material effect upon them in their darkest hour. Had the British been able to get away unscathed, the whole operation might have been reviewed with equanimity if not with satisfaction, but, unhappily, a grave misfortune, arising rather from bad luck than from the opposition of the enemy, came upon the retreating brigades, so that very many of our young sailors after their one week of crowded life came to the end of their active service for the war.

On leaving Antwerp it had been necessary to strike to the north in order to avoid a large detachment of the enemy who were said to be upon the line of the retreat. The boundary between Holland and Belgium is at this point very intricate, with no clear line of demarcation, and a long column of British somnambulists, staggering along in the dark after so many days in which they had for the most part never enjoyed two consecutive hours of sleep, wandered over the fatal line and found themselves in firm but kindly Dutch custody for the rest of the war. Some fell into the hands of the enemy, but the great majority were interned. These men belonged chiefly to three battalions of the 1st Brigade. The 2nd Brigade, with one battalion of the 1st, and the greater part of the Marines, made their way to the trains at St. Gilles-Waes, and were able to reach Ostend in safety. The remaining battalion of Marines, with a number of stragglers of the other brigades, were cut off at Morbede by the Germans, and about half of them were taken, while the rest fought their way through in the darkness and joined their comrades. The total losses of the British in the whole misadventure from first to last were about 2500 men – a high price, and yet not too high when weighed against the results of their presence at Antwerp. On October 10 the Germans under General Von Beseler occupied the city. Mr. Powell, who was present, testifies that 60,000 marched into the town, and that they were all troops of the active army.

It has already been described how the northern ends of the two contending armies were endeavouring to outflank each other, and there seemed every possibility that this process would be carried out until each arrived at the coast. Early in October Sir John French represented to General Joffre that it would be well that the British Army should be withdrawn from the Aisne and take its position to the left of the French forces, a move which would shorten its line of communications very materially, and at the same time give it the task of defending the Channel coast. General Joffre agreed to the proposition, and the necessary steps were at once taken to put it into force. The Belgians had in the meanwhile made their way behind the line of the Yser, where a formidable position had been prepared. There, with hardly a day of rest, they were ready to renew the struggle with the ferocious ravagers of their country. The Belgian Government had been moved to France, and their splendid King, who will live in history as the most heroic and chivalrous figure of the war, continued by his brave words and noble example to animate the spirits of his countrymen.

From this time Germany was in temporary occupation of all Belgium, save only the one little corner, the defence of which will be recorded for ever. Little did she profit by her crime or by the excuses and forged documents by which she attempted to justify her action. She entered the land in dishonour and dishonoured will quit it. William, Germany, and Belgium are an association of words which will raise in the minds of posterity all that Parma, Spain, and the Lowlands have meant to us – an episode of oppression, cruelty, and rapacity, which fresh generations may atone for but can never efface.

The First Battle of Ypres
(Up to the Action of Gheluvelt, October 31)

IT has already been seen that the Seventh Division (Capper's), being the first half of Rawlinson's Fourth Army Corps, had retired south and west after the unsuccessful attempt to relieve Antwerp.

It is not too much to say that in an army where every division had done so well no single one was composed of such fine material as the Seventh. The reason was that the regiments composing it had all been drawn from foreign garrison duty, and consisted largely of soldiers of from three to seven years' standing, with a minimum of reservists. In less than a month from the day when this grand division of 18,000 men went into action its infantry had been nearly annihilated, but the details of its glorious destruction furnish one more vivid page of British military achievement. We lost a noble division and gained a glorious record.

The Third Cavalry Division under General Byng was attached to the Seventh Division, and joined up with it at Roulers upon October 13.

The First Army Corps not having yet come up from the Aisne, these troops were used to cover the British position from the north, the infantry lying from Zandvoorde through Gheluvelt to Zonnebeke, and the cavalry on their left from Zonnebeke to Langemarck from October 16 onwards. It was decided by Sir John French that it was necessary to get possession of the town of Menin, some distance to the east of the general British line, but very important because the chief bridge, by means of which the Germans were receiving their ever-growing reinforcements, was there. The Seventh Division was ordered accordingly to advance upon this town, its left flank being covered by the Third Cavalry Division.

The position was a dangerous one. It has already been stated that the pause on the Aisne may not have been unwelcome to the Germans, as they were preparing reserve formations which might be suddenly thrown against some chosen spot in the Allied line. They had the equipment and arms for at least another 250,000 men, and that number of drilled men were immediately available, some being Landwehr who had passed through the ranks, and others young formations which had been preparing when war broke out. Together they formed no less than five new army corps, available for the extreme western front, more numerous than the whole British and Belgian armies combined. This considerable force, secretly assembled and moving rapidly across Belgium, was now striking the north of the Allied line, debouching not only over the river at Menin, but also through Courtrai, Iseghem, and Roulers. It consisted of the 22nd, 23rd, 24th, 26th, and 27th reserve corps. Of these the 22nd, and later the 24th, followed the Belgians to the line of the Yser, but the other corps were all available for an attack upon the flank of that British line which was faced by formidable opponents – a line which extended over thirty miles and had already been forced into a defensive attitude.

That was the situation when the Seventh Division faced round near Ypres. Sir John French was doing all that he could to support it, and Sir Douglas Haig was speeding up his army corps from the Aisne to take his place to the north of Ypres, but there were some days during which Rawlinson's men were in the face of a force six or seven times larger than themselves.

Upon October 16th and 17th the division had advanced from Ypres and occupied the line already mentioned, the right centre of which rested about the ninth kilometre on the Ypres-Menin road, the order of the brigades from the north being 22nd, 21st, and 20th. On October 18 the division wheeled its left forward. As the infantry advanced, the covering cavalry soon became aware of grave menace from Roulers and Courtrai in the north. A large German force was evidently striking down on to the left flank of the advance. The division was engaged all along the line, for the 20th Brigade upon the right had a brisk skirmish, while the 21st

Brigade in the centre was also under fire, which came especially heavily upon the 2nd Bedfords, who had numerous casualties. About ten o'clock on the morning of the 19th the pressure from the north increased, and the 7th Cavalry Brigade was driven in, though it held its own with great resolution for some time, helped by the fine work of K Battery, R.H.A. The 6th Cavalry Brigade was held up in front, while the danger on the flank grew more apparent as the hours passed. In these circumstances General Rawlinson, fortified in his opinion by the precise reports of his airmen as to the strength of the enemy upon his left, came to the conclusion that a further advance would place him in a difficult position. He therefore dropped back to his original line. There can be little doubt that, if he had persevered in the original plan, his force would have been in extreme danger. As it was, before he could get it back the 1st Welsh Fusiliers were hard hit, this famous regiment losing a major, 5 captains, 3 lieutenants, and about 200 men. The order to retire had failed to reach it, and but for the able handling of Colonel Cadogan it might well have been destroyed.

On October 20, the situation being still obscure, the 20th Brigade carried out a reconnaissance towards Menin. The 2nd Wilts and 2nd Scots Fusiliers, of the 21st Brigade, covered their left flank. The enemy, however, made a vigorous attack upon the 22nd Brigade to the north, especially upon the Welsh Fusiliers, so the reconnaissance had to fall back again, the 1st Grenadier Guards sustaining some losses. The two covering regiments were also hard pressed, especially the Wiltshires, who were again attacked during the night, but repulsed their assailants.

From this time onwards the Seventh Division was to feel ever more and more the increasing pressure as the German army corps from day to day brought their weight to bear upon a thin extended line of positions held by a single division. It will be shown that they were speedily reinforced by the First Corps, but even after its advent the Germans were still able to greatly outnumber the British force. The story from this time onwards is one of incessant and desperate attacks by day and often by night. At first the division was holding the position alone, with the help of their attendant cavalry, and their instructions were to hold on to the last man until help could reach them. In the case of some units these instructions were literally fulfilled. One great advantage lay with the British. They were first-class trained soldiers, the flower of the Army, while their opponents, however numerous, were of the newly raised reserve corps, which showed no lack of bravery, but contained a large proportion of youths and elderly men in the ranks. Letters from the combatants have described the surprise and even pity which filled the minds of the British when they saw the stormers hesitate upon the edge of the trenches which they had so bravely approached, and stare down into them uncertain what they should do. But though the ascendancy of the British infantry was so great that they could afford to disregard the inequality of numbers, it was very different with the artillery. The German gunners were as good as ever, and their guns as powerful as they were numerous. The British had no howitzer batteries at all with this division, while the Germans had many. It was the batteries which caused the terrific losses. It may be that the Seventh Division, having had no previous experience in the campaign, had sited their trenches with less cunning than would have been shown by troops who had already faced the problem of how best to avoid high explosives.

Either by sight or by aeroplane report the Germans got the absolute range of some portions of the British position, pitching their heavy shells exactly into the trenches, and either blowing the inmates to pieces or else burying them alive, so that in a little time the straight line of the trench was entirely lost, and became a series of ragged pits and mounds. The head-cover for shrapnel was useless before such missiles, and there was nothing for it but either to evacuate the line or to hang on and suffer. The Seventh Division hung on and suffered, but no soldiers can ever have been exposed to a more deadly ordeal. When they were at last relieved by the arrival of reinforcements and the consequent contraction of the line, they were at the last pitch of exhaustion, indomitable in spirit, but so reduced by their losses and by the terrific nervous strain that they could hardly have held out much longer.

A short account has been given of what occurred to the division up to October 20. It will now be carried on for a few days, after which the narrative must turn to the First Corps, and show why and how they came into action to the north of the hard-pressed division. It is impossible to tell the two stories simultaneously, and so it may now be merely mentioned that from October 21 Haig's Corps was on the left, and that those operations which will shortly be described covered the left wing of the division, and took over a portion of that huge German attack which would undoubtedly have overwhelmed the smaller unit had it not been for this addition of strength. It is necessary to get a true view of the operations, for it is safe to say that they are destined for immortality, and will be recounted so long as British history is handed down from one generation to another.

On the 21st the enemy got a true conception of the salient in front of the Seventh Division, and opened a vigorous attack, which lasted all day and assumed several different phases at different points. The feature of the morning of the 21st was the severe and, indeed, disastrous artillery fire upon Lawford's 22nd Brigade. The exact range of the British position seems to have been discovered with deadly results. Men, trenches, and machine-guns were all blown to pieces together. The 2nd Warwicks and the 1st Welsh Fusiliers were the two battalions upon which the storm beat hardest, and each of them had some hundreds of casualties. In three days the Welsh Fusiliers, who were on the exposed left flank, lost three-quarters of their effectives, including twenty three of their officers, and yet preserved their military spirit. It became clearer as experience accumulated that the best trenches, if they are once fairly located, can be made untenable or turned into the graves of their occupants by the use of high explosives. The German fire was so severe that it was reckoned that one hundred and twenty shells an hour into or round a trench was a not uncommon rate of fall. The 2nd Queen's also lost seven officers and many men in this day's fighting. In spite of the heavy losses from gunfire the German infantry could make no progress, being held up by a flanking fire of the South Staffords. In the afternoon of October 21 a strong attack was made upon the 21st Brigade in the centre of the line. The brigade was holding a front of two and a half miles, and, although the attack was generally beaten back, a certain number of stormers got through between the trenches and into the woods beyond. Here they lurked for a couple of days, during which time the 2nd Yorkshire Regiment, behind whose line they were lying, were often compelled to have each alternate man facing a different way to keep down the fire. The battalion sent itself reinforcements by hurrying its right company over to help to clear its left. This movement was successful, but was attended with heavy losses, including several officers. Some of the Royal Scots Fusiliers had been forced out of their trenches on the right, and made, under Major Ian Forbes, a gallant attempt to re-establish them, in which Captain Fairlie and many men were lost. The Wiltshires also endured a very severe attack, which they repulsed with great loss to the enemy. On this same eventful day, the 21st, the Second Cavalry Division had been pushed back at Holbeke, and the Germans got round the right flank of the hard-pressed infantry. It was then that General Rawlinson brought his Third Cavalry Division round and established it upon his right instead of his left flank. From this time until October 30 this cavalry division was holding Zandvoorde Ridge, sharing day by day in all the perils and the glories of their comrades of the Seventh Division. There was no more dangerous point than that which was held by the cavalry, and their losses, especially those of the 10th Hussars, were in proportion to the danger. In the course of a few days the Hussars lost Colonel Barnes, Majors Mitford and Crichton and many officers and men.

On October 22 the Second Division of Haig's First Corps, which had been fully occupied to the north with operations which will presently be described, moved down to cover the ground vacated by the Third Cavalry Division and to relieve the pressure upon the infantry of the Seventh Division. The 4th Guards Brigade took its position upon their immediate left. It was time. For four days they had covered the enormous front of eight miles against at least four times their own number, with more than six times their weight of artillery. It was touch and go. They were nearly submerged. It was indeed a vision of joy when the worn and desperate men, looking over their shoulders down the Ypres-Menin road, saw the head of a British column coming swiftly to the rescue. It was the 2nd Highland Light Infantry and the 2nd Worcesters, dispatched from the 5th Brigade, and never was reinforcement more needed. Shortly afterwards further help in the shape of a detachment of the Munster Fusiliers, two troops of the ever-helpful Irish Horse, and one section of artillery appeared upon the scene.

Upon this date (October 22) the 22nd Infantry Brigade of the Seventh Division had fallen back to the railway crossings near Zonnebeke. Thus the salient which the Germans had been attacking was straightened out. Unhappily, the change caused another smaller salient farther south, at the point which was held by the 2nd Wiltshires. On the 22nd and 23rd there was a tremendous shelling of this sector, which was followed on the 24th by an infantry advance, in which the Wiltshires, who had been previously much reduced, were utterly overwhelmed and practically destroyed. The disastrous attack broke upon the British line just after daybreak. The enemy pushed through behind each flank of the Wiltshires, elbowing off the Scots Fusiliers on one side and the Scots Guards on the other. The Germans got in force into the Polygon Woods behind. There were no reserves available save the Northumberland Hussars, a corps which has the honour of being the first British territorial corps to fight for its country. With the aid of some divisional cyclists, this handful of men held back the Germans until the 2nd Warwicks from the north were brought to stem the advance. The Warwicks charged through the wood, their gallant Colonel Loring riding his horse beside them without boot or legging, having been wounded some days before. "Where my men go I go as well," was his answer to medical remonstrance. He was killed by a bullet, but he died at a moment of victory, for his last earthly vision was that of his infantry driving the last Germans out of the wood. Besides their colonel, the regiment lost many officers and men in this fine advance, which was most vigorously supported by the 2nd Worcesters, the only reinforcement within reach. The Worcesters lost 6 officers and 160 men, but did much execution and took a number of prisoners.

At this time the 20th Brigade, being the extreme right of the Seventh Division, held an extended line Brigade. from Kruiseik cross-roads, about a mile east of Gheluvelt village, to near Zandvoorde, with a salient at the village of Kruiseik. On the night of the 25th the Germans planned a furious attack upon the whole salient. The assailants, who were mostly Saxons, broke through the 2nd Scots Guards just north of Kruiseik and got behind the line, which was pushed back for some distance, though Captain Paynter, with the right-hand company, held his position. A counter-attack by the Guards retook the line, together with 200 prisoners, including 7 officers. On the morning of the 26th the Germans were back on them, however, and began by blowing in the trenches of the Border Regiment south of Kruiseik. The German guns had found the exact range of the trenches, and the defenders had the same terrible and intolerable experience which had befallen some of their comrades two days before. It was simply impossible to stand up against the incessant shower of shattering shells. So great was the concussion and the nervous strain that many of the men exposed to it got completely dazed or even became delirious. Grenadiers, Scots Guards, and South Staffords, of the 20th Brigade, held the line until the front trenches were carried by the Germans and many of the occupants made prisoners. It was pitch dark, and it was impossible to tell friend from foe. Major Fraser of the Scots Guards, going forward to reconnoitre, was shot dead and his party was destroyed. A house in a field taken by the Guards yielded no fewer than 200 prisoners, but in the confused fighting in the darkness our losses were greater than our gains. It was in this night-fighting that Lord Dalrymple, Colonel Bolton, and other officers, with some hundreds of men, fell into the hands of the enemy after a most heroic resistance to overpowering numbers and to a weight of artillery which was crushing in its effect. The King's Company of the 1st Grenadiers was isolated and in great danger, but managed to link up with the British line. The 1st South Staffords also lost some hundreds of men, and was only saved by fine handling on the part of Colonel Ovens. Kruiseik was abandoned, and a new line taken up half a mile farther back. It was a critical night, during which the energy and firmness of General Capper were splendidly employed in reforming and stiffening his sorely tried division. On the 26th the 20th Brigade, which had been so heavily hit the day before, was drawn out of the line for a rest, and the two other brigades closed up to cover a shorter line. The work of the 20th at Kruiseik had been magnificent, but their losses were appalling, including their Brigadier, Ruggles-Brise, who was wounded. Here, for the instant, we shall leave the Seventh Division, though their ordeal was by no means done, and we shall turn to those other forces which had been forming in the northern or Ypres section of the long battle line.

The reader will remember, if he casts his mind back, that the whole British line, as it extended from the south about October 18, consisted of the Second Corps and the advance guard of the Indians near La Bassée; then, in succession, the Third Corps in the Armentières district, the First Cavalry and Second Cavalry near Messines and Wytschaete, the Seventh Division near Gheluvelt, and finally the Third Cavalry on their left, joining up with the French, who carried the line to where the Belgians were reforming on the Yser. The First Corps had detrained from the Aisne, and was concentrated between St. Omer and Hazebrouck upon October 18 and 19. They represented a last British reserve of about thirty-five thousand men to set against the large new armies who were advancing from the north. The urgent question to be decided was where they should be placed, since there were so many points which needed reinforcement.

Sir John French has explained in his dispatch the reasons which swayed him in deciding this question.

"I knew," he said, "that the enemy were by this time in greatly superior strength upon the Lys and that the Second and Third Cavalry and Fourth Corps were holding a much wider front than their strength and numbers warranted. Taking these facts alone into consideration, it would have appeared wise to throw the First Corps in to strengthen the line, but this would have left the country north and east of Ypres and the Ypres Canal open to a wide turning movement by the Third Reserve Corps and at least one Landwehr Division which I knew to be operating in that region. I was also aware that the enemy was bringing large reinforcements up from the east, which could only be opposed for several days by two or three French cavalry divisions, some French Territorials, and the Belgian Army."

He proceeds to state his opinion that the Belgian Army was in no condition to withstand unsupported such an attack, and that if it were allowed to sweep past us it was very likely to wash away all opposition before it, and get into the Channel ports in our rear. With this consideration in his mind, Sir John French took the bold and dangerous, but absolutely necessary, step of leaving the long, thin, thirty-mile line to do the best it could, and prolonging it by another ten or twelve miles by forming up the First Corps on the same alignment, so as to present as long a British breakwater as possible to the oncoming flood. There was nothing else to be done, and the stronger the flood the more need there was to do it, but it is safe to say that seldom in history has so frail a barrier stood in the direct track of so terrible a storm.

In accordance with this resolution, Haig's First Corps moved, on October 20, through Poperinghe and Ypres and took their place upon the north or left side of the Seventh Division. On their own left in this position was the French cavalry corps of General de Mitry, while the Third Division of British cavalry was on their right. As the movement commenced Sir John French had a personal interview with General Haig, in which he held out hopes that the greater part of the new German levies had been deflected to hold our southern advance, and that he would only find the Third Reserve Corps and some Landwehr in front of him to the north of Ypres. His object was to advance upon the line of Bruges and drive the enemy towards Ghent. Meanwhile the gallant little Belgian army, which was proving itself a glutton at fighting, was entrenched along the line of the Ypres Canal and the Yser River, where they held their own manfully in spite of all that they had endured.

The first large landmark in the direction of Bruges was Thorout, and towards this the First Corps, with the Third Cavalry Division upon its right, took its first steps, little thinking that it was butting forward against an approaching army of at least double its own strength. It was very quickly made to realise its position, however, and any dreams of a victorious entry into Bruges were speedily dispelled. Only too fortunate would it be if it could hold its own line without retreat and disaster. Upon the 21st Haig's men attacked Poel-Chapelle and Passchendaale, French cavalry and Territorials (the Eighty-seventh and Eighty-ninth Divisions) under General Bidon advancing on their left, while the Seventh Division, as already described, kept pace upon its right. There was strong opposition from the first, but the corps advanced in spite of it until the pressure from the north became too severe for the French, whose flank was exposed to the full force of it.

The British attack upon the morning in question was planned as follows. The Second Division was to advance upon Passchendaale. The First had orders to take Poel-Chapelle. The latter movement was headed by the 3rd Brigade, who were directed by General Landon to go forward about nine o'clock, the 1st Queen's having the station for their objective while the 1st South Wales Borderers attacked the village. The 1st Gloucesters were in reserve. The enemy met the attack with shell-fire, which it was

French troops on the march.

difficult to locate, as the country was flat and enclosed. The progress of the movement, however, was steady though slow. About ten o'clock there were signs of a considerable hostile infantry advance from the north. The attack, however, made good progress up to midday, when there was a general retirement of the French Territorials, followed later by the French cavalry upon the British left. They moved back towards Bixschote. The Gloucester Regiment, who had been thrown out to reinforce that flank, were also driven back, and were in turn reinforced by the Coldstream Guards. This battalion executed a bayonet charge in clearing the small village of Koekuit, but later on had to retire, finding their flank exposed. It should be mentioned that one French corps, the Seventh Cavalry Division, kept its position upon the British left, and it is also only fair to point out that as the German advance was mainly from the north, it was upon the left flank, covered by the French, that it would fall. The 1st Camerons were now dispatched to the flank to stiffen the French resistance, taking up their position near the inn which is midway upon the road between Steenstraate and Langemarck, north of the village of Pilken – an inn with which they were destined to have stirring associations. With the support of the 46th Battery, the Highlanders held up a German brigade which was thrusting through behind our main line; but farther west, in the Steenstraate direction, the defence against a northern advance was miserably thin, consisting only of one company of the Sussex Regiment and the 116th Battery. In the circumstances the more success Haig's troops attained in front, and the more they advanced, the more dangerous was their position upon the flank.

About 2:30 the German advance from the north became more formidable, and the 1st South Welsh Borderers, between Langemarck and Poel-Chapelle, were heavily counter-attacked and suffered considerable loss, between two and three hundred in all. Two companies of the 2nd Welsh were pushed up to their help. It was clear, however, that the advance could not be continued. The 1st Brigade was therefore ordered to hold the line between Steenstraate and Langemarck, with their centre at the inn north of Pilken, so as to face the German advance from the north. Then from Langemarck the British line turned southwards, being carried on for two miles by the 3rd Brigade to hold the enemy who were coming from the east. The 2nd Brigade was in reserve at Boesinghe. During this long and difficult day the Second Division, operating upon the right of the First, was not subjected to the same anxiety about its flank. It advanced upon its objective in the face of severe opposition, ending more than once in a brief bayonet encounter. Several counter-attacks were made by the Germans, but they were all beaten back with loss. About two o'clock, however, the Second Division learned of the flank pressure which was holding up the First Division, and also of the extreme need for help experienced by the 22nd Brigade of the Seventh Division on their right. In these circumstances it was necessary to abandon the idea of further advance and to send south those reinforcements, the opportune arrival of which has been already described.

As a net result of the two days' operations General Haig was not able to attain the line of Passchendaale – Poel-Chapelle, as originally planned, but he gained sufficient ground to establish himself from Langemarck to Zonnebeke, more than half-way to his objective. The whole character of the operations during these days was more of the familiar British type, being conducted upon the surface of the earth rather than under it, and cavalry making its last appearance for many a long day. Many fine deeds of valour were done. In one of these Captain Rising, of the Gloucester Regiment, with ninety men, defended some point with such heroic tenacity that when, some days afterwards, the Brigadier attempted to get the names of the survivors for commendation not one could be found. Quaintly valorous also is the picture of Major Powell, of the North Lancashires, leading his wing with a badly-sprained ankle, and using a cottage chair for a crutch, upon which he sat down between rushes. It is hopeless, however, and even invidious to pick instances where the same spirit animated all. The result was definite. It had been clearly shown that the enemy were in considerably greater strength than had been imagined, and instead of a rearguard action from weak forces the British found themselves in the presence of a strong German advance.

All day large forces of the enemy were advancing from Roulers and were impinging upon different points of the Franco-British line. These troops were composed of partially-trained men, volunteers and reservists, but they attacked with the utmost determination, and endured heavy losses with great bravery. It is a remarkable proof of the elaborate preparations for war made by Germany that, behind all their original gigantic array, they still had ready within the country sufficient arms and uniforms to fit out these five new army corps. He who plans finds it easy to prepare, and whoever will compare this profusion of munitions in Germany with the absolute lack of them in the Allied countries will have no further doubt as to which Government conspired against the peace of the world.

On October 21, Sir John French began to feel that there were new factors in his front. In the evening, at a meeting with Haig and Rawlinson, he discussed the unexpected strength of the German reinforcements and admitted that the scheme of an advance upon Bruges would become impossible in the face of such numbers. Intelligence reports indicated that there was already a German army corps in front of each British division. General Joffre had promised considerable French reinforcements upon October 24, and all that could be done was for the British troops to hold their ground to the last man and to resist every pressure until the equality of the forces could be restored. Could they hold the line till then? That was the all-important question.

October 22 was the first day of that long ordeal of incessant attacks which the First Corps was called upon to endure, until by constant attrition it had become almost as worn as the Seventh Division to the south. On this day the German attack, which attained the full volume of later days, spent itself here and there along the extended lines. Only at one point did the enemy have some success, which, however, was the prelude to disaster.

The line from Steenstraate to Langemarck, defending the British left flank, was held by the 1st Brigade, the Scots Guards upon the extreme left, then the Cameron Highlanders, and the Black Watch in reserve. In the middle of the line north of Pilken was a solitary inn, already mentioned, round which trenches had been cut in horse-shoe fashion, the concavity of the shoe pointing southwards. This point marked the junction between the Camerons and the Scots Guards. About 3 P.M. this position was driven in and captured by a sudden and determined advance of the enemy. The German charge was a fine feat of arms, for it was carried out largely by *Einjährige*, who may be roughly compared to the Officers' Training Corps of our British system. These high-spirited lads advanced singing patriotic songs, and succeeded in carrying the trenches in the face of soldiers who are second to none in the British Army – soldiers, too, who had seen much service, while the German cadets were new to the work. The performance was much appreciated by British officers and men.

The Black Watch endeavoured without success to restore the line, and the 1st Northamptons were called upon from divisional reserve, while from all parts troops converged towards the gap. On the arrival of the Northamptons they pushed up towards the interval which, now existed between the Scots Guards and the remains of the Camerons, but found the gap broader than had been thought, and strongly occupied. It was then evening, and it was thought best to delay the counter-attack until morning and so have time to bring up reinforcements. The 1st North Lancashires and the 2nd South Staffords were accordingly ordered up, together with the 1st Queen's Surrey and the 2nd Rifles, the whole operation being under the immediate command of General Bulfin. The advance began at six in the morning, over very difficult ground which had been barb- wired during the night. The progress was slow but steady, and at eleven o'clock an assault upon the inn was ordered. The position was critical, since the enemy was now firmly lodged in the very centre of the flank of the British position, and was able to enfilade all the trenches of the First Division. The Queen's Surrey, the 2nd King's Royal Rifles, and the 1st North Lancashires charged home with splendid energy, capturing the trenches round the inn, besides releasing sixty Camerons and taking over five hundred prisoners. The trenches were carried by the North Lancashires, led by Major Carter. It was the second time within six weeks that this battalion had made a decisive bayonet charge. The price paid was six officers and 150 men. The inn itself was rushed by Captain Creek's company of the Queen's, while Major Watson, of the same regiment, organised the final advance. The fighting at this point was not finished for the day. In the late evening the enemy, with fine tenacity of purpose, attacked the inn once more and drove the Queen's out of a salient. The line was then straightened on each side of the inn and remained firm. Both the attack on the inn and the defence of the line were splendidly supported by the field artillery.

Whilst the 1st Brigade had in this fashion got into and out of a dangerous position, there had been a severe attack upon two regiments of Landon's 3rd Brigade stationed at Langemarck. The defending units were the 2nd Welsh Regiment and the 1st Gloucesters. Aided by a strong artillery backing, they beat off these attacks and inflicted a very heavy loss upon the enemy. The Allied line to the north was solid and unbroken.

The British losses during these operations of the First Corps amounted to 1500 men, while those of the Germans were exceedingly heavy. These inexperienced troops advanced with an indiscriminating enthusiasm which exposed them to severe retaliation. It is doubtful if at any time in the campaign the British fire found so easy a mark. One thousand five hundred dead were counted in the vicinity of Langemarck, and the total loss (including over six hundred prisoners) could not have been less than 10,000 men. Correspondence afterwards captured showed that the Twenty- third Reserve Corps sustained such losses that for a time at least it was out of action. The Twenty-seventh Reserve Corps was also hard hit. A letter from a soldier in the 246th Regiment mentions that only eighty men were left of his battalion after the action of the 24th.

On October 24 and 25 the arrival of French reinforcements allowed the British to shorten up their defensive line, which had been unduly extended. The Seventeenth Division of the Ninth French Army Corps took over the line of the Second Division, which was drawn back to St. Jean, and in turn took over part of the front of the Seventh Division. French territorial troops, under General de Mitry, relieved the First British Division on the line Hannebeke – Langemarck–Steenstraate. The First Division was drawn back to Zillebeke.

Meantime the Second Division, having the Ninth Corps upon its left and the Seventh Division upon its right, made an attack towards Bacelaer, taking two guns and some prisoners. This advance was renewed upon the 26th, this being the day upon which, as already described, the Germans pushed back the 20th Brigade of the Seventh Division at the Kruiseik salient, creating a situation which brought the Second Division to a standstill.

In this movement forward of the Second Division from October 24 to 26, the Guards' 4th Brigade were on the right, the 6th Brigade on the left, with the French to the left of them. The 5th Brigade were in reserve. Two small villages were taken by storm, the Germans being driven out of loopholed houses, though at a considerable cost of officers and men. It was in this operation that Colonel Bannatyne, the gallant leader of the 1st King's Liverpool, was killed. Ten other officers and several hundred men of this corps were killed or wounded. The 1st Berkshires, fighting to the left of the King's, shared in its losses and in its success. The Irish Guards were held up before Reutel and separated from the rest of the force, but managed to extricate themselves after some anxious hours.

On October 27, Sir John French came in person to Hooge, at the rear of the fighting line, and inquired into the state of the hard-pressed troops. He found the Seventh to be now such a skeleton division that it was thought best to join it with Haig's First Corps, forming one single command.

The attendant Third Cavalry Division was also attached to the First Corps. These readjustments took place upon October 27. They were, of course, of a temporary character until the eagerly awaited Eighth Division should arrive and so give General Rawlinson a complete Fourth Corps. At present there was a very immediate prospect that half of it might be annihilated before the second half appeared. The general arrangement of this section of the battlefield was now as depicted, the Seventh Division being entirely south of the Ypres – Menin roadway.

And now the great epic of the first Battle of Ypres was rising to its climax, and the three days of supreme trial for the British Army were to begin. Early upon October 29, a very heavy attack developed upon the line of the Ypres-Menin road. There is a village named Gheluvelt, which is roughly half-way upon this tragic highway. It lay now immediately behind the centre of the British line. About half a mile in front of it the position ran through the important cross-roads which lead to the village of Kruiseik, still in the British possession. The line through the Kruiseik cross-roads was that which was furiously assailed upon this morning, and the attack marked the beginning of a great movement to drive in the front continuing throughout the 30th and culminating in the terrible ordeal of the 31st, the crisis of the Ypres battle and possibly of the Western campaign.

FitzClarence's 1st Brigade lay to the north of the road, and the battered, much-enduring 20th Brigade upon the south. They were destined together to give such an example of military tenacity during that day as has seldom been equalled and never exceeded, so that the fight for the Kruiseik crossroads may well live in history amongst those actions, like Albuera and Inkermann, which have put the powers of British infantry to an extreme test. The line was held by about five thousand men, but no finer units were to be found in the whole Army. The attack was conducted by an army corps with the eyes of their Emperor and an overpowering artillery encouraging them from the rear. Many of the defending regiments, especially those of the 20th Brigade, had already been terribly wasted. It was a line of weary and desperate men who faced the German onslaught.

The attack began in the mists of the early morning. The opening was adverse to the British, for the enemy, pushing very boldly forward upon a narrow front and taking full advantage of the fog, broke a way down the Menin road and actually got past the defending line before the situation was understood. The result was that the two regiments which flanked the road, the 1st Black Watch and the 1st Grenadiers, were fired into from behind and endured terrible losses. Among the Grenadiers Colonel Earle, Majors Forrester and Stucley, Lord Richard Wellesley, and a number of other officers fell, while out of 650 privates only 150 were eventually left standing. The 2nd Gordons, upon the right of the Grenadiers, suffered nearly as heavily, while the 1st Coldstream, upon the left of the Black Watch, was perhaps the hardest hit of all, for at the end of that dreadful day it had not a single officer fit for duty. The right company of the 1st Scots Guards shared the fate of the Coldstream. The line was pushed back for a quarter of a mile and Kruiseik was evacuated, but the dead and wounded who remained in the trenches far exceeded in numbers those who were able to withdraw.

Two small bodies who were cut off by the German advance did not fall back with their comrades, and each of them made a splendid and successful resistance. The one near Kruiseik was a mixed party under Major Bottomley of the 2nd Queen's West Surrey. The other was C Company of the 2nd Gordons under Captain B.G.R. Gordon and Lieutenant Laurence Carr. These small islands of khaki, in the midst of a broad stream of grey, lay so tight and fired so straight that they inflicted very great damage upon the enemy, and were able to hold their own, in ever-diminishing numbers, until under the protection of darkness the survivors regained the British line.

In the meantime, a number of small dashing counter-attacks by the indomitable infantry was bringing the British line forward again. South of the road the Gordons, under Colonel Uniacke, dashed themselves again and again against the huge host which faced them, driving them back, and then in their turn recoiling before the ponderous advance of the army corps. They were maddened by the sound of the rolling fire ahead of them, which showed that their own C Company was dying hard. In one of these counter-attacks Captain Brooke brought every straggler into the fray, and died while trying to cut his way through to his comrades. To the north of the road Captain Stephen, with the remains of the 1st Scots Guards, threw themselves upon the German flank and staggered it by their fire. The Germans, who had almost reached Gheluvelt, were now worried in this way on either flank, while the 2nd Border battalion and the Welsh Borderers with the rallied remains of the broken regiments were still facing them in front. The enemy was held, was stricken front and flank with a murderous fire, and recoiled back down the Menin road.

Imperial eyes and overmastering guns were equally powerless to drive them through that iron defence. Five thousand British soldiers had driven back an army corps, but had left more than half their number upon the scene of victory.

The Second Division, to the north of the road in the direction of Reutel, had been ordered to counter-attack, and the other brigades of the Seventh Division to the south did the same. While Haig had a man standing he was ready to hit back. Between these two flanking forces there was a movement in the centre to follow the Germans back and to recover some of the lost ground. Landon's Third Brigade, less the Gloucester Regiment, was pushed forward. These troops moved past Gheluvelt and advanced along the line of the road, the 1st Queen's, their right-hand unit, linking up by a happy chance with their own 2nd Battalion, who were now on the left of the 22nd Brigade of the Seventh Division. Left of the Queen's were the 2nd Welsh to the immediate south of the main road, while to their left again lay the 1st South Wales Borderers, in front of the village of Gheluvelt. By evening these troops had recovered some of the ground, but the village of Kruiseik, which had always constituted a salient, was now abandoned. The cross-roads also remained in the hands of the enemy. Landon's Brigade continued to bar the further German advance preparing in stern resignation for the renewed and heavier blow which all knew to be in readiness, and which was destined two days later to bring them a glorious annihilation.

It was clear upon the evening of the 29th that serious mischief was afoot, for there were great signs of movement on the German side, and all night, the continual rattle of wheels was heard to the eastward. These menacing sounds were actually caused by a very strong reinforcement, the Fifteenth German Corps (Strasburg) of the regular army, which, followed by the Thirteenth Corps and the Second Bavarian Corps, were coming into the battle line with the declared intention of smashing their way through to Ypres. Correspondence, afterwards captured, showed that the German Emperor had issued a special appeal to these troops, declaring that the movement was one which would be of decisive importance to the war. It was, of course, not the venerable town of Ypres which had assumed such a place in the mind both of the Emperor and his people, but it was Calais and the Channel coast to which it was the door. Once in the possession of these points, it seemed to their perfervid minds that they would be in a position to constrain Great Britain to an ignominious peace, a course which would surely have ruined the cause of the Allies and placed the whole world under the German heel. No less was the issue at stake. The British Army from Langemarck in the north to La Bassée in the south were resolutely determined that the road was barred, while to left and to right they had stout-hearted comrades of Belgium and of France.

At half-past six upon October 30 a very heavy attack developed, which involved the whole line of the First Corps and also the French Ninth Corps upon its left. This attack upon the left was carried out by the Reserve Corps 26 and 27, with whom we had had previous dealings, and it was repulsed with considerable loss by the French and the 6th British Brigade. To the south, however, the British were very violently engaged down the whole line of trenches from the position of the Seventh Division near the Ypres-Menin road, through Zandvoorde, where the Third Cavalry Division was holding on under great difficulties, and on southward still, past the position of the Second Cavalry down to Messines, where the First Cavalry Division was also heavily engaged. The front of battle was not less than twelve miles in length, with one continuous long-drawn rattle of small arms and roar of guns from end to end.

The British may have anticipated that the chief blow would fall at the same spot as had been attacked the day before. As a matter of fact, it was directed farther south, at Zandvoorde, on the immediate right of the Seventh Division.

The first sign of success for the strenuous German efforts upon October 30 was the driving in of Kavanagh's 7th Guards' Cavalry Brigade from their trenches at the Zandvoorde Ridge. On this ridge, which is not more than a hundred and twenty feet high, the Germans concentrated so tremendous and accurate a fire that the trenches were in many places demolished and became entirely untenable. The survivors of the Life

Guards and Blues who made up this brigade withdrew steadily through the reserve trenches, which were held by the 6th cavalry Brigade, and reformed at Klein Zillebeke in the rear. Two squadrons, however, and Lord Worsley's machine-gun section were killed or taken by the assailants. The unoccupied trenches were seized by the Sixth Bavarian Reserve Division, who advanced rapidly in order to improve their advantage, while their artillery began to pound the reserves. The cavalry had been strengthened, however, by the Greys and 3rd Hussars upon the left, while the 4th Hussars lined up on the right, and C, I, and K Horse Artillery batteries vigorously supported. In spite of great pressure, the position was held. Farther south the First Cavalry Division was also at very close grips with the Twenty-sixth Division of the Thirteenth German Army Corps, and was hard put to it to hold its own. Along the whole cavalry position there was extreme strain. A squadron of the 1st Royals were forced to evacuate the château of Holebeke, and the line in this quarter was pushed back as far as St. Eloi, thus flattening a considerable salient.

The danger of a position which consists of so long a line with few reserves is that any retirement at any point immediately exposes the flanks of the neighbouring units to right and left. Thus the evacuation of Zandvoorde threw open the right flank of the Seventh Division, even as its left had been in the air upon the day before. On getting through, the Germans were on the right rear of the 1st Welsh Fusiliers and enfiladed them badly, destroying all the officers and a first considerable proportion of the regiment, which had already been greatly reduced. Colonel Cadogan was among those who fell. The 22nd Brigade was forced to fall back, and the 2nd Yorkshires and 2nd Scots Fusiliers, of the 21st Brigade, being left in a salient, suffered heavily, especially the latter battalion, the conduct of which from first to last was remarkable even among such men as fought beside them. These two regiments held on with the greatest determination until orders to retire reached them, which were somewhat belated, as several orderlies were killed in bringing them. The 2nd Bedfords, who had themselves sustained very severe losses from the German artillery fire, covered the retirement of the remains of these two gallant units. The

Seventh Division then covered the line from the canal through Klein Zillebeke and along the front of the woods to near Gheluvelt.

The position was now most critical. The Germans were in possession of Zandvoorde Ridge on the British right flank, a most important position whence guns could command a considerable area. Ypres was only four miles distant. There was nothing but a line of weary and partially broken infantry to protect the flank from being entirely pierced. The whole of a German active army corps was attacking upon this line. The order was given to hold the new positions at all costs, but on the evening of the 30th the situation was full of menace for the morrow. The German flood was still thundering against the barrier, and the barrier seemed to be giving. At about 2 P.M. on October 30 the 1st Irish Guards and the 2nd Grenadiers, who were in reserve to two battalions of the Coldstream in trenches in the Polygon Wood, near Reutel Village, were ordered to help the Seventh Division. General Capper subsequently directed them to take the place of the cavalry on the right of his division. The Irish Guards were accordingly on the right of the Seventh Division from now onwards, and the Grenadiers were on their right, extending down to the canal in front of Klein Zillebeke. The commander of the Ninth French Corps also, with that fine loyalty which his comrades have shown again and again during the war, easing many a difficult and perhaps saving some impossible situations, put three battalions and some cavalry at the disposal of the British. Two regiments of Bulfin's 2nd Brigade were also brought across and thrust into the gap. But the outlook that evening was not cheering. The troops had been fighting hard for two days without a break. The losses had been heavy. The line had been driven back and was greatly strained. It was known that the Germans were in great strength and that the attack would be renewed on the morrow. The troops and their leaders faced the immediate future in a spirit of sombre determination.

During the 30th Landon's Brigade had strengthened their position near Gheluvelt, and General Haig, realising that this was the key of his line, moved up the 2nd King's Royal Rifles and the 1st North Lancashires to form a reserve under the orders of General Landon. These regiments took a position south-west of Gheluvelt and connected up more closely between the Seventh Division and the 3rd Brigade of the First Division. It was well that a closely-knitted line had been formed, for at the dawn of day upon the 31st a most terrific attack was made, which was pushed with unexampled fierceness during the whole day, falling chiefly upon the centre and left of the Seventh Division and upon the 1st Queen's and 2nd Welsh of the Third Brigade.

A weak point developed, unfortunately, in the front line, for the Seventh Division in its enfeebled condition was further weakened by forming somewhat of a salient in the Kruiseik direction. They behaved with all their usual magnificent gallantry, but they were not numerous enough to hold the ground. The line was broken and the remains of the 2nd Royal Scots Fusiliers, after being exposed to heavy fire from 5:30 A.M., were outflanked and surrounded in the early afternoon. The bulk of the survivors of this battalion had been sent to reinforce the line elsewhere, but the remainder, some sixty in number, were killed, wounded, or taken, including their gallant colonel, Baird Smith, who had been hit the day before. The Picton tradition which disregards wounds unless they are absolutely crippling was continually observed by these stern soldiers. On the left of the Scots Fusiliers the 2nd Bedfords were also involved in the catastrophe, but drew off with heavy losses.

The left wing of the Seventh Division began to retire, and the 1st Queen's upon the right of the 3rd Brigade had both their flanks turned and were reduced to a handful under Major Watson and Lieutenant Boyd, who still held together as a unit. It was a great morning in the history of this regiment, as the two battalions had fought side by side, and their colonels, Pell and Coles, had both fallen in the action.

The line of the 3rd Brigade had been drawn up across the Menin road some four hundred yards to the east of the village. The road itself was held by the 2nd Welsh Regiment, supported by the 54th Battery (Major Peel), which was immediately behind the village. Both the battalion and the battery fought desperately in a most exposed situation. The Welsh Regiment were driven out of their trenches by a terrific shell-fire followed by an infantry attack. They lost during the day nearly six hundred men, with sixteen officers, killed, wounded, or missing. Colonel Morland was killed and Major Prichard badly wounded. Finally, after being pushed back, holding every possible point, they formed up under Captain Rees across the open in a thin skirmishing line to cover the battery, which was doing great work by holding back the German advance. One German gun was in action upon the Menin road. Lieutenant Blewitt took a British gun out on to the bare road to face it, and a duel ensued at five hundred yards, which ended by the German gun being knocked out at the third shot by a direct hit.

When the First Division at the centre of the British line were driven in, as already described, and the Seventh Division were pushed back into the woods, the situation became most critical, for there was a general retirement, with a victorious enemy pressing swiftly on upon the British centre. The men behaved splendidly, and the officers kept their heads, taking every opportunity to form up a new line. The 2nd Rifles and 1st North Lancashires in immediate support of the centre did all that men could to hold it firm. The German artillery lengthened their range as the British fell back, and the infantry, with their murderous quick-firers scattered thickly in the front line, came rapidly on. Communications were difficult, and everything for a time was chaos and confusion. It looked for an hour or two as if Von Deimling, the German leader, might really carry out his War Lord's command and break his road to the sea. It was one of the decisive moments of the world's history, for if the Germans at that period had seized the Channel ports, it is difficult to say how disastrous the result might have been both to France and to the British Empire. At that moment of darkness and doubt a fresh misfortune, which might well have proved overwhelming, came upon the hard-pressed forces. About 1:30 a shell exploded in the headquarters at the château of Hooge, and both General Lomax, of the First Division, and General Munro, of the Second, were put out of action, the first being wounded and the second rendered unconscious by the shock. It was a brain injury to the Army, and a desperately serious one, for besides the two divisional commanders the single shell had killed or wounded Colonels Kerr and Perceval, Major Paley, Captains Ommany and Trench, and Lieutenant Giffard. General Landon, of the 3rd Brigade, took the command of the First Division at a moment's notice, and the battle went forward. A line was hurriedly formed, men digging as for their lives, whilst broken units threw themselves down to hold off the rolling grey wave that thundered behind. The new position was three-quarters of a mile back and about four hundred yards in advance of Veldhoek, which is the next village down the Ypres road. The Seventh Division had also been rolled back, but the fiery Capper, their divisional chief, who has been described as a British Samurai, was everywhere among his regiments, reforming and bracing them.

The British soldiers, with their incomparable regimental officers, rose to the crisis, whilst General Haig was behind the line at Hooge, directing and controlling, like a great engineer who seeks to hold a dam which carries an overpowering head of water. By three o'clock the new line was firmly held.

Now General Haig, seeking round for some means of making a counter-attack, perceived that on his left flank he had some reserve troops who had been somewhat clear of the storm and might be employed. The 2nd Worcesters were ordered to advance upon Gheluvelt, the initiative in this vital movement coming from General FitzClarence of the 1st Brigade. On that flank the troops had not joined in the retirement, and, including the South Wales Borderers of the 3rd Brigade, were still in their original trenches, being just north of the swathe that had been cut in the British line, and just south of where the Second Division, extended to cracking point, with one man often for every eight or nine feet, and no supports, were defending the left flank of the Army.

When the village of Gheluvelt and the trenches to the north of it had been captured by the enemy, a gap had been left of about five hundred yards between the northern edge of the village and these South Wales Borderers. This gap the 2nd Worcesters were ordered to fill. They were in reserve at the time in the south-west corner of the Polygon Wood, but on being called upon they made a brilliant advance under Major Hankey. One company (A) was detached to guard the right flank of the advance. The other three companies came on for a thousand yards. At one point they had to cross two hundred and twenty yards of open under heavy shrapnel-fire. One hundred men fell, but the momentum of the charge was never diminished. Their rapid and accurate fire drove back the German infantry, while their open order formation diminished their own losses. Finally they dashed into the trenches and connected up the village with the line of the Welsh Borderers. Their right platoons, under Captain Williams, held the village until nearly midnight. Altogether the advance cost the battalion 187 casualties, including 3 officers, out of 550 who were in the ranks that day. Up to dusk the Worcesters were exposed to heavy shrapnel fire, and small detached parties of the enemy came round their right flank, but their position was strengthened and strongly held until the final readjustment of the line. It was a fine advance at a critical moment, and did much to save the situation. The whole movement was strongly supported by the guns of the 42nd Battery, and by some of the 1st Scots Guards upon the left of the Welsh Borderers.

It has been stated that a line had been formed near Veldhoek, but this difficult operation was not performed in an instant, and was rather the final equilibrium established after a succession of oscillations. The British were worn to a shadow. The 2nd Queen's had 2 officers and 60 men left that night, the 2nd Welsh had 3 officers and 93 men. Little groups, who might have been fitted into a large-sized drawing-room, were settling a contention upon which the fate of the world might depend. But the Germans also had spent all their force. The rattle of musketry behind their advance was enough to tell them that the British were still in their trenches, and the guns were for ever playing on them with deadly effect. Gradually they began to dissolve away among the thick woods which flank the road. They were learning that to penetrate the line of a resolute adversary is not necessarily the prelude to victory. It may mean that the farther you advance the more your flanks are exposed. So it was now, when the infantry to the north on one side and the Third Cavalry

Division on the other were closing in on them. That long tentacle which was pushing its way towards Ypres had to be swiftly withdrawn once more, and withdrawn under a heavy fire from the 29th, 41st, and 45th field batteries.

The Scattered German infantry who had taken refuge in the woods of Hooge, which lie to the south of the road, were followed up by mounted and dismounted men of the Royals, 10th Hussars, and 3rd Dragoon Guards, aided by some French cavalry. These troops advanced through the woods, killing or taking a number of the enemy. By nightfall the Germans had fallen back along the whole debated line; the various British units, though much disorganised, were in close touch with each other, and the original trenches had in the main been occupied, the Berkshire Regiment helping to close the gap in the centre. The flood had slowly ebbed away, and the shaken barrier was steady once more, thanks to the master-hands which had so skilfully held it firm. The village of Gheluvelt remained in the hands of the Germans, but the British trenches were formed to the west of it, and the road to the sea was barred as effectually as ever. These are the main facts of the action of Gheluvelt, which may well be given a name of its own, though it was only one supremely important episode in that huge contention which will be known as the First Battle of Ypres.

In the southern portion of the Ypres area at Klein Zillebeke a very sharp engagement was going on, which swung and swayed with as much violence and change as the main battle on the Menin road. The German attack here was hardly inferior in intensity to that in the north. Having pushed back Lawford's weak brigade (22nd) it struck full upon part of Bulfin's 2nd Brigade, which had been detached from the First Division and sent to cover the right of the Seventh Division. Its own flank was now exposed, and its situation for a time was critical. The German advance was sudden and impetuous, coming through a wood which brought the dense mass of the enemy's leading formation almost unseen right up to the British line. The position of the 2nd Brigade was pierced, and the two regiments present, the 2nd Sussex and the 1st Northamptons, were driven back with loss. Their brigadier rallied them some hundreds of yards to the rear, where they formed up into a skirmish line in the open, and, though unable to advance, kept back the Germans with their rifle-fire. The losses still continued, however, and the enemy came on again and again with numbers which seemed inexhaustible. Suddenly there was a charging yell from behind a low slope covering the rear, and over the brow there appeared some three hundred survivors of the 2nd Gordons, rushing at full speed with fixed bayonets. At the same moment the dismounted troopers of the 6th Cavalry Brigade and a company of sappers ran forward to join in the charge. The whole British force was not one to three of its opponents, but as the reinforcing line swept on, cheering with all its might, the survivors of the hard-pressed brigade sprang up with a shout and the united wave burst over the Germans. Next moment they had broken and were flying for their lives through the Zwartelen Wood. The pursuit lasted for some distance, and a great number of the enemy were bayoneted, while several hundreds were taken prisoners.

There have been few more critical occasions in British operations than this action upon October 31, when the Germans so nearly forced their way to Ypres. It is the peculiarity of modern warfare that, although vast armies are locked in a close struggle, the number of men who can come into actual contact at any one point is usually far more limited than in the old days, when each host could view the other from wing to wing. Thus the losses in such an action are small as compared with the terrific death-roll of a Napoleonic battle. On the other hand, when the operations are viewed broadly and one groups a series of actions into one prolonged battle, like the Aisne or Ypres, then the resulting losses become enormous. The old battle was a local conflagration, short and violent. The new one is a widespread smoulder, breaking here and there into flame. In this affair of Gheluvelt the casualties of the British did not exceed 2000 or 3000, while those of the Germans, who were more numerous and who incurred the extra loss which falls upon the attack, could not have been less than twice that figure. One thousand five hundred dead were actually picked up and six hundred prisoners were taken. Some hundreds of prisoners were also taken by the enemy. The British artillery, which worked desperately hard all day, had many losses both upon the 30th and the 31st. The 12th Battery had all its guns silenced but one, and many others were equally hard hit.

On the night of the 31st considerable French reinforcements began to arrive, and it was high time that they did so, for the First Corps, including the Seventh Division, were likely to bleed to death upon the ground that they were holding. It had stood the successive attacks of four German corps, and it had held its line against each of them. But its own ranks had been grievously thinned and the men were weary to death. The strain, it should be added, was equally great upon the Ninth French Corps to the north, which had its own set of assailants to contend with. Now that the line of the Yser, so splendidly guarded by the Belgians, had proved to be impregnable, and that the French from Dixmude in the north had repulsed all attacks, the whole German advance upon Calais, for which Berlin was screaming, was centred upon the Ypres lines. It was time, then, that some relief should come to the hard-pressed troops. For several days the French on the right and the left took the weight of the attack upon themselves, and although the front was never free from fighting, there was a short period of comparative rest for Haig's tired men. In successive days they had lost Kruiseik, Zandvoorde, and Gheluvelt, but so long as they held the semicircle of higher ground which covers Ypres these small German gains availed them nothing.

Looking back at the three actions of the 29th, a great 30th, and especially of the 31st of October, one can clearly perceive that it was the closest thing to a really serious defeat which the Army had had since Le Cateau. If the Germans had been able to push home their attack once again, it is probable that they would have taken Ypres, and that the results would have been most serious. Sir John French is reported as having said that there was no time in the Mons retreat when he did not see his way, great as were his difficulties, but that there was a moment upon October 31 when he seemed to be at the end of his resources. To Sir John at Ypres converged all the cries for succour, and from him radiated the words of hope and encouragement which stiffened the breaking lines. To him and to his untiring lieutenant, Douglas Haig, the Empire owed more that day than has ever been generally realised. The latter was up to the firing line again and again rallying the troops. The sudden removal of the two divisional commanders of the First Corps was a dreadful blow at such a moment, and the manner in which General Landon, of the 3rd Brigade, took over the command of the First Division at a moment's notice was a most noteworthy performance. The fact that three divisions of infantry with brigades which resembled battalions, and battalions which were anything from companies to platoons, destitute of reserves save for a few dismounted cavalry, barred the path to a powerful German army, is one of the greatest feats of military history. It was a very near thing. There was a time, it is said, when the breech-blocks had actually been taken from the heavy guns in order to disable them, and some of the artillery had been passed back through Ypres. But the line held against all odds, as it has done so often in the past. The struggle was not over. For a fortnight still to come it was close and desperate. But never again would it be quite so perilous as on that immortal last day of October, when over the green Flemish meadows, beside the sluggish water-courses, on the fringes of the old-world villages, and in the heart of the autumn-tinted woods, two great Empires fought for the mastery.

Such was the British epic. There was another to the north which was no less wonderful, and which will be celebrated by the poets and historians of the lands to which the victors belong. It will tell of the glorious stand during this critical ten days of the Belgians, so weary, so battered, and yet so indomitable. It will tell how they made head against the hosts of the Duke of Würtemberg, and how in the end they flooded their own best land with the salt water which would sterilise it in order to cover their front. It will tell also of the splendid Frenchmen who fought at Dixmude, of Ronarch with his invincible marines, and of Grossetti, the fat and debonair, seated in an armchair in the village street and pointing the road to victory with his cane. Not least, perhaps, in that epic will be the tale of the British monitors who, with the deadly submarines upon one side of them and the heavy German batteries upon the other, ran into the Flemish coast and poured their fire upon the right flank of the attacking Germans. Ten days the great battle swung and swayed, and then here as at Ypres the wave of the invaders ebbed, or reached its definite flood. It would be an ungenerous foe who would not admit that they had fought bravely and well. Not all our hatred of their national ideals nor our contempt for their crafty misleaders can prevent us from saluting those German officers and soldiers who poured out their blood like water in the attempt to do that which was impossible.

The First Battle of Ypres (continued)
(From the Action of Gheluvelt to the Winter Lull)

WHILST this severe fighting had been going on to the north of the British position, the centre, where the first dismounted cavalry were holding the line of trenches, was so terribly pressed that it is an extraordinary thing that they were able to hold their own. The Second Corps, which at that time had just been withdrawn for a rest from the La Bassée lines, were the only available reinforcements. When news was flashed south as to the serious state of affairs, two regiments, the 2nd Yorkshire Light Infantry and the 2nd Scottish Borderers from the 13th Infantry Brigade, were sent up in motor-buses by road to the relief. Strange indeed was the sight of these vehicles flying along the Flemish roads, plastered outside with the homely names of London suburbs and crammed with the grimy, much-enduring infantry. The lines at Messines were in trouble, and so also were those at Wytschaete farther to the north. To this latter place went two battalions of Shaw's 9th Brigade, the 1st Northumberland Fusiliers and the 1st Lincolns. Hard work awaited the infantry at Messines and at Wytschaete, for in both places Allenby's troopers were nearly rushed off their feet.

It has already been shown that on October 30 a severe assault was made upon the Third Cavalry Division, when the 7th Brigade (Kavanagh's) was forced out of Zandvoorde by the Fifteenth German Army Corps. Upon this same date a most strenuous attack, made in great force and supported by a terrific shell-fire, was directed along the whole line of the cavalry from Wytschaete to Messines. No British troops have been exposed to a more severe ordeal than these brave troopers, for they were enormously outnumbered at every point, and their line was so thin that

An English bus, this one captured by German troops.

it was absolutely impossible for them to prevent it from being pierced by the masses of infantry, from the Twenty-fourth Corps and Second Bavarian Corps, which were hurled against them. From the extreme left of the Second Cavalry Division near Wytschaete to the right of the First Cavalry Division south of Messines the same reports came in to the anxious General, of trenches overwhelmed or enfiladed, and of little isolated groups of men struggling most desperately to keep a footing against an ever-surging grey tide which was beating up against them and flowing through every gap. In the north Gough's men were nearly overwhelmed, the 5th Irish Lancers were shelled out of a farmhouse position, and the 16th Lancers, shelled from in front and decimated by rifles and machine-guns from the flank, were driven back for half a mile until three French battalions helped the line to reform. The pressure, however, was still extreme, the Germans fighting with admirable energy and coming forward in never-ending numbers.

An Indian regiment of the 7th (Ferozepore) Brigade, the 129th Baluchis, had been helping the cavalry in this region since October 23, but their ranks were now much decimated, and they were fought almost to a standstill. Two more British regiments from the Second Corps, the 1st Lincolns and the 1st Northumberland Fusiliers of the 9th Brigade, together with their Brigadier, Shaw, who was a reinforcement in himself, were, as already stated, hurried off from the south in motor-buses to strengthen Gough's line. Advancing into what was to them an entirely strange position these two veteran regiments sustained very heavy losses, which they bore with extreme fortitude. They were surprised by the Germans on the road between Kern in el and Wytschaete on the night of October 31, the same night upon which the London Scottish to the south of them were so heavily engaged. Colonel Smith succeeded in extricating the Lincolns from what was a most perilous position, but only after a loss of 16 officers and 400 men. The Fusiliers were almost as hard hit. For forty-eight hours the battle swung backwards and forwards in front of Wytschaete, and in the end the village itself was lost, but the defensive lines to the west of it were firmly established. By November the second strong French reinforcements had appeared, and it was clear that this desperate attempt to break through the very centre of the British position had definitely failed.

The struggle at Messines, some five miles to the south, had been even more severe and sanguinary than at Wytschaete. In the early morning of the 31st the Bays and the 5th Dragoon Guards upon the left of the Messines position, after a heavy shell-fire, were driven out of their trenches by a sudden furious advance of the German infantry. The front of the village of Messines was held by Wild's 57th Rifles, who were driven in by the same attack, every officer engaged being killed or wounded. A reserve company of Wild's Rifles and a squadron of the 5th Dragoon Guards endeavoured to restore the fight, but could not hold the torrent. The 9th Lancers, also in front of the village and to the right of the Indians, held on for a long time, repulsing the infantry attacks, until they were driven back by the deadly shell-fire. At one time they were enfiladed on both sides and heard the Germans roaring their war-songs in the dark all round them; but they were able, owing to the coolness of Colonel Campbell and the discipline of his veteran troopers, to fall back and to reform upon the western side of the village. Lance-Corporal Seaton distinguished himself by covering the retreat of his whole squadron, remaining single-handed in his trench until his maxim was destroyed, after he had poured a thousand shots into the close ranks of his assailants.

The situation was so serious after dawn upon the 31st that General De Lisle had to call for help from Wilson's Fourth Infantry Division, holding the line upon his right. The Inniskilling Fusiliers were extended so as to relieve his right flank. The struggle within Messines was still going forward with fighting from house to house, but the Germans, who were coming on with overpowering numbers and great valour, were gradually winning their way forward. The Oxfordshire Hussars, fresh from the base, were thrown into the combat. A second line of defence had been arranged a mile or so to the west, near Wulverghem, but if Messines must go the victors should at least pay the price down to the last drop of blood which could be wrung from them. Reinforcements were within sight, both French and British, but they were scanty in quantity though superb in quality. It was a most critical position, and one cannot but marvel at the load of responsibility which Sir John French had to bear upon this day, for from the left of Haig's First Corps in the north down to Neuve Chapelle in the south, a stretch of twenty-five miles, there was hardly a point which was not strained to the verge of cracking. Cool and alert, he controlled the situation from his central post and threw in such reinforcements as he could find, though, indeed, they could only be got by taking them from places where they were wanted and hurrying them to places where they were needed even more urgently. He was strengthened always by the knowledge that General Joffre behind him was doing all that a loyal colleague could to find fresh columns of his splendid infantrymen to buttress up the hard-pressed line.

For the moment, however, none of these were available, and Messines was still partly in British, partly in German hands. Briggs's 1st Brigade – Bays, 5th Dragoon Guards, and 11th Hussars – with the Oxfords, held on to the western edge of the town. To their left, linking up with Gough's men in the Wytschaete sector, was the 4th Dragoon Guards. Late in the afternoon the 2nd Scots Borderers and the 2nd Yorkshire Light Infantry the joint detachment under Major Coke, arrived from the south, and were at once advanced upon Messines to stiffen the defence. Under heavy fire they established themselves in the village. Evening fell with desperate street fighting and the relative position unchanged. Twice the Bavarians stormed into the central square, and twice they fell back after littering it with their bodies. It seemed hopeless to hold the village against the ever-growing pressure of the Germans, and yet the loss of the village entailed the loss of the ridge, which would leave a commanding position in the hands of the enemy. Village and ridge were mutually dependent, for if either were lost the other could not be held.

As it proved, it was the ridge and not the village which could no longer sustain the pressure. On the night of October 31 Mullen's 2nd Cavalry Brigade – 9th Lancers, 4th Dragoon Guards, and 11th Hussars – took over the defence from Briggs. Of these, the 4th Dragoon Guards were to the left of the village upon the ridge. The London Scottish had been brought up,

German prisoners at Messines.

and they were placed upon the left of the 4th Dragoon Guards, forming a link of the defence which connected up the Second Cavalry Division with the First. The right-hand regiment of the latter, the 6th Carbineers, of Bingham's 4th Brigade, were upon the left of the London Scottish. These two regiments held the centre of the ridge. The London Scottish had already suffered considerable losses. Hurried up from the lines of communication to St. Eloi, they were pushed forward at once into action, and were exposed for hours to all the nerve-racking horrors of a heavy shell-fire endured in most insufficient trenches. A more severe ordeal was in store for them, however, during the grim night which lay before them. The admirable behaviour of Colonel Malcolm's men excited the more attention as they were the first Territorial infantry to come into action, and they set a standard which has been grandly sustained by the quarter-million of their comrades who have from first to last come into the line.

On the early morning of November 1 there had been a strong attempt within the village to improve the British position, and some ground was actually gained by the cavalrymen, the Yorkshire Light Infantry, and the Scots Borderers. What occurred, however, on the ridge to the north made all further effort a useless waste of life. The Bavarian infantry had come with an irresistible rush against the thin British line. The order to hold their ground at all costs was given, and the London Scots answered it in a way which gained the highest praise from the many soldiers who saw it. It is not claimed that they did better than their Regular comrades. That would be impossible. The most that can be said is that they proved themselves worthy to fight in line with them. After being exposed for several hours to heavy shell-fire, it was no light task for any troops to be called upon to resist a direct assault. From nine in the evening of October 31 to two in the morning, under the red glare of burning houses. Colonel Malcolm's Scottish and Colonel Annesley's Carbineers held back the Bavarian advance, an advance which would have meant the piercing of the British line. At two o'clock the Bavarians in greatly predominant force were all round the Scots, and even the reserve companies found work for their bayonets, preventing the enemy from encircling their companions.

The losses were very heavy – 400 men and 9 officers, including their gallant doctor, McNab, who was villainously stabbed as he bandaged a patient. In spite of the great pressure, the ground was held all night, and it was not till dawn, when the regiment found that it was outflanked on both sides and nearly surrounded, that, under cover of the fire of E Battery R.H.A., it fell back. The Carbineers and the Scots were close together, and the Germans, with their usual quick ingenuity, approached the former with a cry of "We are the London Scots." A disaster might have occurred in the darkness but for the quickness and bravery of a young officer, Lieutenant Hope Hawkins, who rushed forward, discovered the identity of the Germans, and fell, riddled with bullets, even while he gave warning to his comrades.

The Germans had won the ridge, but the British line was still intact and growing stronger every hour. The village was held by the Scots Borderers and Yorkshiremen until nearly ten o'clock, when they were ordered to fall back and help to man the new line. The shock had been a rude one, but the danger-hour was past here as in the north.

The fateful November 1 had come and gone. The villages of Messines and Wytschaete were, it is true, in German hands, but French reinforcements of the Sixteenth Corps were streaming up from the south, the line, though torn and broken, still held firm, and the road to Calais was for ever blocked. There was still pressure, and on November 2 the 11th Hussars were badly cut up by shell-fire, but the line was impregnable. Sir John French summed up in a few terse words the true meaning of the operations just described, when he said afterwards, in addressing the 9th Lancers, "Particularly I would refer to the period, October 31, when for forty-eight hours the Cavalry Corps held at bay two German army corps. During this period you were supported by only three or four battalions, shattered and worn by previous fighting, and in so doing you rendered inestimable service." There have been few episodes in the war which have been at the same time so splendid and so absolutely vital. The First Cavalry Division lost 50 per cent of its numbers between October 30 and November 2, and the Second Division was hardly in better case, but never did men give their lives to better purpose. Their heroism saved the Army.

Meanwhile the current of operations was evidently running strongly towards the northern end of the British line, where help was badly needed, as Haig's men had been fought almost to exhaustion. There was no British reinforcement available save only the weary Second Corps, the remains of which from this date began to be drafted northwards. It was already known that the German Emperor had appeared in person in that region, and that a great concentration of his troops was taking place. At the same time the French were making splendid exertions in order to stiffen their own line and help us in those parts, like Messines, Wytschaete, and Ploegsteert, where the attack was most formidable. It was a great gathering towards the north, and clearly some hard blows were to be struck. Northwards then went General Morland, of the Fifth Division, taking with him four more weak battalions. The whole line had moved upwards towards the danger spot, and these troops now found themselves east of Bailleul, close to the village of Neuve Église. For the moment General Smith-Dorrien was without an army, for half his men were now supporting General Willcocks in the south and half General Allenby or General Haig in the north.

The British leaders all along the line were, as usual, desperately endeavouring to make one man do the work of three, but they were buoyed up by the knowledge that good Father Joffre, like some beneficent earthly Providence, was watching over them from the distance, and that fresh trainfuls of his brave little men were ever steaming into the danger zone. Day by day the line was thickening and the task of the Kaiser becoming more difficult. It was hoped that the crisis was past. If our troops were exhausted so also, it was thought, were those of the enemy. We could feel elated by the knowledge that we had held our ground, while they could hardly fail to be depressed by the reflection that they had made little progress in spite of so many heroic efforts, and that Calais was as far from them as ever.

The narrative must now return to the defenders of the Ypres approaches, who were left in a state of extreme exhaustion by the critical action of October 31. On November 1 the First Corps was not in a condition to do more than to hold its line. This line was now near to Veldhoek, to the west of Gheluvelt village, and to that extent the Germans had profited by their desperate fighting, but this was a detail of small consequence so long as an unbroken British Army covered the town that was still the objective of the enemy. The Ninth French Corps to the north of the British had lost heavily, but to the south of the canal lay the Sixteenth French Corps, which was in comparatively good condition. This corps now made an advance to take some of the pressure off the British line, while Moussy's regiments to the north of the canal were to co-operate with Bulfin's men upon their left. Upon the left of Bulfin's 2nd Brigade were two battalions of the 4th Brigade of Guards.

One of these battalions had a terrible experience upon this morning. For some reason the trenches of the Irish Guards were exposed to an enfilading fire from the high explosives of the Germans, which wrought even more than their customary damage. For hours the Guardsmen lay under a terrific fire, to which they could make no reply, and from which they could obtain no protection. When at last, in the afternoon, they were compelled to fall back, their losses had been great, including their colonel, Lord Ardee, 7 other officers, and over 300 men. It is the hard fate of the side which is weaker in artillery to endure such buffetings with no possibility of return.

The French attack of the Sixteenth Corps had been brought to a speedy standstill, and a severe counter-attack, preceded by a heavy shell-fire, had fallen upon General Moussy's men and upon the half of the 2nd Brigade. Help was urgently needed, so the remains of the 7th Brigade from the Third Cavalry Division were hurried forward. The Germans were now surging up against the whole right and right-centre of the line. It seems to have been their system to attack upon alternate days on the right and on the centre, for it will be remembered that it was on October 29 that they gained the Gheluvelt cross-roads, and on October 31 Gheluvelt village, both in the centre, while on October 30 they captured the Zandvoorde ridge upon the British right, and now, on November 1, were pressing hard upon the right once more.

That morning the Army sustained a loss in the person of General Bulfin, who was wounded in the head by shrapnel. Fortunately his recovery was not a lengthy one, and he was able to return in January as commander of the Twenty-eighth Division. Upon his fall, Lord Cavan, of the 4th Brigade, took over the command upon the hard-pressed right wing. At half-past one the hundred survivors of the 2nd Gordons, on the right of the Seventh Division, and the 2nd Oxford and Bucks, were desperately hard pressed by a strong German infantry advance, and so were the remains of the Sussex and Northamptons. The only available help lay in the 23rd Field Company of Royal Engineers. Our sappers proved, as they have so often done before, that their hearts are as sound as their heads. They pushed off the enemy, but incurred heavy losses. The situation was still critical when at the summons of Lord Cavan the 2nd Grenadiers advanced and cleared the Germans from the woods in the front and flank, while the 10th Hussars supported their advance. A gap had been left in the trenches from which the Irish Guards had been pushed, but this was now filled up by cavalry, who connected up with the French on their right and with the Guards upon their left. The general effect of the whole day's fighting was to drive the British line farther westward, but to contract it, so that it required a smaller force. Two battalions – the Gordons and the Sussex – could be taken out and brought into reserve. The centre of the line had a day's rest and dug itself into its new positions, but the units were greatly mixed and confused.

November 2 brought no surcease from the constant fighting, though the disturbance of these days, severe as it was, may be looked upon as a mere ground swell after the terrific storm of the last days of October.

On the morning of the 2nd the Ninth French Corps upon the British left, under General Vidal, sent eight battalions forward to the south and east in the direction of Gheluvelt. Part of this village was actually occupied by them. The Germans meanwhile, with their usual courage and energy, were driving a fresh attack down that Menin road which had so often been reddened by their blood. It was the day for a centre attack on their stereotyped system of alternate pushes, and it came duly to hand. An initial success awaited them as, getting round a trench occupied by the Rifles, they succeeded in cutting off a number of them. The 3rd Brigade was hurried up by General Landon to the point of danger, and a French Zouave regiment helped to restore the situation. A spirited bayonet charge, in which the Gloucesters led, was beaten back by the enemy's fire. After a day of confused and desultory fighting the situation in the evening was very much as it had been in the morning. Both that night and the next day there was a series of local and sporadic attacks, first on the front of the Second Division and then of the Seventh, all of which were driven back. The Germans began to show their despair of ever gaining possession of Ypres by elevating their guns and dropping shells upon the old Cloth Hall of that historic city, a senseless act of spiteful vandalism which exactly corresponds with their action when the Allied Army held them in front of Rheims.

November 4 was a day of menaces rather than of attacks. On this day, units which had become greatly mixed during the incessant and confused fighting of the last fortnight were rearranged and counted. The losses were terrible. The actual strength of the infantry of the First Division upon that date was: 1st Brigade, 22 officers, 1206 men; 2nd Brigade, 43 officers, 1315 men; 3rd Brigade, 27 officers, 970 men; which make the losses of the whole division about 75 per cent. Those of the Second Division were very little lighter. And now for the 25 per cent remainder of this gallant corps there was not a moment of breathing space or rest, but yet another fortnight of unremitting work, during which their thin ranks were destined to hold the German army, and even the Emperor's own Guard, from passing the few short miles which separated them from their objective. Great was the "will to conquer" of the Kaiser's troops, but greater still the iron resolve not to be conquered which hardened the war-worn lines of the soldiers of the King.

November 5 was a day of incessant shell-fire, from which the Seventh Division, the 4th and the 6th Brigades were the chief sufferers. On this day the Seventh Division, which had now been reduced from 12,000 infantry to 2333, was withdrawn from the line. In their place were substituted those reinforcements from the south which have already been mentioned. These consisted of eleven battalions of the Second Corps under General McCracken; this corps, however, was greatly worn, and the eleven battalions only represented 3500 rifles. The Seventh Division was withdrawn to Bailleul in the south, but Lawford's 22nd Brigade was retained in corps reserve, and was destined to have one more trial before it could be spared for rest. The day was memorable also for a vigorous advance of the Gloucester Regiment, which was pushed with such hardihood that they sustained losses of nearly half their numbers before admitting that they could not gain their objective.

A description has been given here of the events of the north of the line and of the cavalry positions, but it is not to be supposed that peace reigned on the south of this point. On the contrary, during the whole period under discussion, while the great fight raged at Ypres, there had been constant shelling and occasional advances against the Third Corps in the Armentières section, and also against the Indians and the Second Corps down to the La Bassée Canal.

The most serious of these occurred upon November 9. Upon this date the Germans, who had knocked so loudly at Messines and at Wytschaete without finding that any opening through our lines was open to them, thought that they might find better luck at Ploegsteert, which is a village on the same line as the other two. Wytschaete is to the north, Messines in the middle, and Ploegsteert in the south, each on the main road from Ypres to Armentières, with about four miles interval between each. The German attack was a very strong one, but the hundredfold drama was played once more. On the 3rd Worcesters fell the brunt, and no more solid fighters have been found in the Army than those Midland men from the very heart of England. A temporary set-back was retrieved and the line restored. Major Milward, of the Worcesters, a very gallant officer, was grievously wounded in this affair. The counter-attack which restored the situation was carried out mainly by the 1st East Lancashires, who lost Major Lambert and a number of men in the venture.

Upon November 6, about 2 P.M., a strong German advance drove in those French troops who were on the right of Lord Cavan's Brigade

– 4th – which occupied the extreme right of Haig's position. The point was between Klein Zillebeke and the canal, where a German lodgment would have been most serious. The retirement of the French exposed the right flank of the 1st Irish Guards. This flank was strongly attacked, and for the second time in a week this brave regiment endured very heavy losses. No. 2 company was driven back to the support trenches, and No. 1 company, being isolated, was destroyed. Their neighbours on the left, the 2nd Grenadiers stood fast, but a great and dangerous alley-way was left for the Germans round the British right wing. The situation was splendidly saved by Kavanagh's 7th Cavalry Brigade, who galloped furiously down the road to the place where they were so badly needed. This hard-worked *corps d'élite*, consisting of the 1st and 2nd Life Guards supported by the Blues, now dismounted and flung themselves into the gap, a grimy line of weather-stained infantry with nothing left save their giant physique and their spurs to recall the men who are the pride of our London streets. The retiring French rallied at the sight of the sons of Anak. An instant later the Germans were into them, and there was a terrific *mêlée* of British, French, and Prussians, which swung and swayed over the marshland and across the road. Men drove their bayonets through each other or fired point-blank into each other's bodies in a most desperate fight, the Germans slowly but surely recoiling, until at last they broke. It was this prompt and vigorous stroke by Kavanagh's Brigade which saved a delicate situation. Of the three cavalry regiments engaged, two lost their colonels – Wilson of the Blues and Dawnay of the 2nd Life Guards. Sixteen officers fell in half an hour. The losses in rank and file were also heavy, but the results were great and indeed vital. The whole performance was an extraordinarily fine one.

Early on the morning of November 7 Lawford's 22nd Brigade, which was now reduced to 1100 men, with 7 officers, was called upon to retake a line of trenches which the enemy had wrested from a neighbouring unit. Unbroken in nerve or spirit by their own terrific losses, they rushed forward, led by Lawford himself, a cudgel in his hand, carried the trench, captured three machine-guns, held the trench till evening, and then retired for a time from the line. Captains Vallentin and Alleyne, who led the two regiments into which the skeleton brigade had been divided, both fell in this feat of arms. After this action there remained standing the brigadier, 3 officers, and 700 men. The losses of the brigade work out at 97 per cent of the officers and 80 per cent of the men, figures which can seldom have been matched in the warfare of any age, and yet were little in excess of the other brigades, as is shown by the fact that the whole division on November 7 numbered 44 officers and 2336 men. It is true that many British regiments found themselves in this campaign with not one single officer or man left who had started from England, but these were usually the effects of months of campaigning. In the case of the Seventh Division, all these deadly losses had been sustained in less than three weeks. Britain's soldiers have indeed been faithful to the death. Their record is the last word in endurance and military virtue.

The division was now finally withdrawn from the fighting line. It has already been stated that there were reasons which made its units exceptionally fine ones. In General Capper they possessed a leader of enormous energy and fire, whilst his three brigadiers – Watts, Lawford, and Ruggles-Brise – could not be surpassed by any in the Army. Yet with every advantage of officers and men there will always be wonder as well as admiration for what they accomplished. For three days, before the First Corps had come thoroughly into line, they held up the whole German advance, leaving the impression upon the enemy that they were faced by two army corps. Then for twelve more days they held the ground in the very storm-centre of the attack upon Ypres. When at last the survivors staggered from the line, they had made a name which will never die.

The bulk of Smith-Dorrien's Corps had now been brought north, so that from this date (November 7) onwards the story of the First and Second Corps is intimately connected. When we last saw this corps it will be remembered that it had been withdrawn from the front, having lost some twelve thousand men in three weeks of La Bassée operations, and that the Indian Corps had taken over their line of trenches. Such fighting men could not, however, be spared in the midst of such a fight. The hospital was the only rest that any British soldier could be afforded. Whilst they had still strength to stand they must line up to the German flood or be content to see it thunder past them to the coast. They were brought north, save only Bowes' 8th Brigade and Maude's 14th, which remained with the Indians in the south. Although the Seventh Division had been drawn out of the line, its attendant cavalry division still remained to give its very efficient help to General Haig.

The British position, though by no means secure, was getting stronger day by day, for General d'Urbal of the Eighth French Army to the north, and General Maud'huy to the south, had both been strongly reinforced, and with their usual good comradeship did all they could to strengthen the flanks and shorten the front of the British line.

The men of the Second Corps who had come north from the La Bassée district were not left long unmolested in their new sphere of operations. On the afternoon of November 7 there was a hot German attack upon that portion of the line which had just been vacated by the Seventh Division. The trenches were now held by the Fifth Division (Morland's).

The enemy may have hoped for some advantage from a change which they may well have observed, but they found that, though the units might be different, the same old breed still barred their path. On this occasion, after the early rush had spent itself upon the 1st Lincolns, it was the 2nd West Ridings who led the counter-charge. The line, however, was never fully re-established. A number of smaller attacks broke upon the front of the Second Division on the same day, leaving a few score of prisoners behind them as they ebbed. On the same day, November 7, the enemy got into the trenches of the 2nd Highland Light Infantry and remained in them, for all of them were bayoneted or taken. Upon this day the London Scottish were brought up into the Ypres line – a sign, if one were needed, that after the action described they were accepted as the peers of their comrades of the Regular Army, for no empty compliments are passed when the breaking of a unit may mean the enfilading of a line.

November 8 was a quiet day, but it was well known from every report of spy, scout, and aeroplane to be the lull before the storm. One German brigade came down the Menin road, and went up it again, leaving a hundred dead on or beside the causeway. This attack inflicted some loss upon the 1st North Lancashires and on the 1st Scots Guards. The 1st Bedfords captured a trench that night. The 9th and the 10th were uneventful, and the tired troops rested on their arms, though never free for an hour from the endless pelting of shells. To the north and east the Eagles were known to be gathering. There were the Emperor, the Emperor's Guard, and a great fresh battle of the Germans ready for one grand final dash for Calais, with every rifle in the firing line and every cannon to support it. Grave messages came from headquarters, warning words were passed to anxious brigadiers, who took counsel with their colonels as to fire-fields and supports. Batteries were redistributed, depleted limbers refilled, and observation posts pushed to the front, while the untiring sappers gave the last touches to traverse and to trench. All was ready for the fray. So close were the lines that at many points the conversations of the enemy could be heard.

The Germans had already concentrated a large number of troops against this part of the British line, and they were now secretly reinforced by a division of the Prussian Guard. Documents found afterwards upon the dead show that the Guard had had special orders from the Emperor to break the line at all costs. The brigades which attacked were made up of the 1st and 2nd Foot Guards, the Kaiser Franz Grenadiers No. 2, the Königin Augusta Grenadiers No. 4, and the battalion of Garde Jäger – 13,000 men in all. It was to be victory or death with the *corps d'élite* of the German army, but it was no less victory or death with the men who opposed them. After an artillery preparation of appalling intensity for three hours along the line of both the First and Second Divisions, the infantry advance began about 9:30 on the morning of November 11 amid a storm of wind and rain. They are gregarious fighters, the Germans, finding comfort and strength in the rush of serried ranks. Even now the advance was made in a close formation, but it was carried out with magnificent dash, amazing valour, and a pedantic precision which caused, for example, the leading officers to hold their swords at the carry. The Prussian Guardsmen seemed to have lost nothing, and also to have learned nothing, since their famous predecessors lay dead in their ranks before St. Privat, forty-four years before. The attack was directed against the front of the two divisions of the First British Army Corps, but especially on the 1st Brigade, so that Guardsman faced Guardsman, as at Fontenoy. There were none of the chivalrous greetings of 1745, however, and a stern hatred hardened the hearts of either side. The German Guard charged on the north of the Menin road, while a second advance by troops of the line was made upon the south, which withered away before the British fire. Nothing could stop the Guards, however. With trenches blazing and crackling upon their flank, for the advance was somewhat diagonal, they poured over the British position and penetrated it at three different points where the heavy shells had overwhelmed the trenches and buried the occupants, who, in some cases, were bayoneted as they struggled out from under the earth. It was a terrific moment. The yells of the stormers and the shrill whistles of their officers rose above the crash of the musketry-fire and roar of the guns. The British fought in their customary earnest silence, save for the short, sharp directions of their leaders. "They did not seem angry – only business-like," said a hostile observer. The troops to the immediate north of the Menin road, who had been shelled out of their trenches by the bombardment, were forced back and brushed aside into the woods to the north, while the Germans poured through the gap. The 4th Royal Fusiliers of the 9th Brigade, upon the right of the point where the enemy had penetrated, were enfiladed and lost their gallant colonel, MacMahon, a soldier who had done great service from the day of Mons, and had just been appointed to a brigade. The regiment, which has worked as hard and endured as great losses as any in the campaign, was reduced to 2 officers and 100 men.

The German Guard poured on into the woods which lay in the immediate rear of the British position, but their formation was broken and the individualism of the Briton began to tell. Next to MacMahon's regiment lay the 1st Scots Fusiliers, sister battalion to that which had been destroyed upon October 31. With fierce joy they poured volleys into the flank of the Guard as the grey figures rushed past them into the woods. Four hundred dead Germans were afterwards picked out from the underwood at this point. The Scots Fusiliers were also hard hit by the German fire.

At this period the Germans who had come through the line had skirted the south of a large wood of half-grown trees, called the Polygon Wood, and had advanced into the farther one, named Nonnebusch. At this point they were close to the British artillery, which they threatened to overwhelm. The 41st Brigade R.F.A., and especially the 16th Field Battery, were in the immediate line of their advance, and the gunners looking up saw the grey uniforms advancing amid the trees. Colonel Lushington, who commanded the artillery brigade, hurriedly formed up a firing line under his adjutant, composed partly of his own spare gunners and partly of a number of Engineers, reinforced by cooks, officers' servants, and other odd hands who are to be found in the rear of the army, but seldom expect to find themselves in the van of the fight. It was a somewhat grotesque array, but it filled the gap and brought the advance to a halt, though the leading Germans were picked up afterwards within seventy yards of the guns. Whilst the position was critical at this point of the front, it was no less so upon the extreme right, where the French detachment, who still formed a Link between the canal on the south and the British right flank, were shelled out of their trenches and driven back. Lord Cavan's 4th Brigade, their nearest neighbours, were too hard pressed to be able to help them. To the north of the Menin road a number of British units were intact, and these held up the German flood in that region. There are two considerable woods – the Polygon to the north and the Nonnebusch to the south-west of the Polygon – the edges of which have defined the British position, while their depths have harboured their artillery. Now the 1st King's Liverpool Regiment held firm to the south of the Polygon Wood, while north of them were the 2nd Highland Light Infantry, with a field company of Engineers. Farther to the south-west were the 1st Connaught Rangers, while on the other side of the Nonnebusch road was the 7th Cavalry Brigade. In the afternoon of this day the enemy, skirting the south of the Polygon Wood, had actually entered the Nonnebusch Wood, in which it faced the artillery as already described. In the Polygon Wood, when they penetrated the trenches of the 1st Brigade, they had the Bang's Liverpool Regiment on their right, which refused to move, so that for a long time the Prussian Guard and the King's lay side by side with a traverse between them. "Our right is supported by the Prussian Guard," said the humorous adjutant of the famous Lancashire regiment. While the main body of the Guard passed on, some remained all day in this trench.

The German Guardsmen had been prevented from submerging the 41st Brigade of Artillery, and also the 35th Heavy Battery, by the resistance of an improvised firing line. But a more substantial defence was at hand. The 2nd Oxford and Bucks Light Infantry, which had been in divisional reserve near Ypres, had been brought forward and found itself at Westhoek, near the threatened guns. This regiment is the old 52nd, of the Peninsular Light Division, a famous corps which threw itself upon the flank of Napoleon's Guard at Waterloo and broke it in the crisis of the battle. Once again within a century an Imperial Guard was to recoil before its disciplined rush. Under Colonel Davies the regiment swept through the wood from north-west to south-east, driving the Germans, who had already been badly shaken by the artillery fire, in a headlong rout. Many threw down their arms. The loss to the Oxfords was surprisingly small, well under fifty in all. As they emerged from the wood they were joined by some of the 1st Northamptons from the 2nd Brigade upon the right, while on the left there was a rush of Connaughts and Highland Light Infantry from their own (Haking's) brigade and of Engineers of the 25th Field Company, who showed extraordinary initiative and gallantry, pushing on rapidly, and losing all their officers save one and a number of their men without flinching for an instant. A party of the Gloucesters, too, charged with the Northamptons upon the right, for by this time units were badly mixed up, as will always happen in woodland fighting. "It was all a confused nightmare," said one who tried to control it. The line of infantry dashed forward, a company of the Oxfords under Captain H. M. Dillon in the lead, and the khaki wave broke over a line of trenches which the Germans had taken, submerging all the occupants. There was another line in front, but as the victorious infantry pushed forward to this it was struck in the flank by a fire from French batteries, which had been unable to believe that so much progress could have been made in so short a time.

It was now nearly dark, and the troops were in the last stage of exhaustion. Of the 1st Brigade something less than 400 with 4 officers could be collected. It was impossible to do more than hold the line as it then existed. Two brave attempts were made in the darkness to win back the original front trenches, but it could not be done, for there were no men to do it. Save for one small corner of the Polygon Wood, the Germans had been completely cleared out from the main position. At twelve and at four, during the night, the British made a forward movement to regain the advanced trenches, but in each case the advance could make no progress. At the very beginning of the second attempt General FitzClarence, commanding the 1st Brigade, was killed, and the movement fizzled out. Besides General FitzClarence, the Army sustained a severe loss in General Shaw of the 9th Brigade, who was struck by a shell splinter, though happily the wound was not mortal. The German losses were exceedingly severe: 700 of their dead were picked up within a single section of the British line, but the main loss was probably sustained in the advance before they reached the trenches. Killed, wounded, and prisoners, their casualties cannot have been less than 10,000 men.

It was a fine attack, bravely delivered by fresh troops against weary men, but it showed the German leaders once for all that it was impossible to force a passage through the lines. The Emperor's Guard, driven on by the Emperor's own personal impetus, had recoiled broken, even as the Guard of a greater Emperor had done a century before from the indomitable resistance of the British infantry. The constant fighting had reduced British brigades to the strength of battalions, battalions to companies, and companies to weak platoons, but the position was still held. They had, it is true, lost about five hundred yards of ground in the battle, but a shorter line was at once dug, organised, and manned. The barrier to Ypres was as strong as ever.

The strain upon the men, however, had been terrific. "Bearded, unwashed, sometimes plagued with vermin, the few who remained in the front line were a terrible crew," says the American, Coleman. "They were like fierce, wild beasts," says another observer. They had given their all, almost to their humanity, to save Britain. May the day never come when Britain will refuse to save them.

Glancing for a moment down the line to the south, there had been continuous confused contention during this time, but no great attack such as distinguished the operations in the north. Upon November 7 two brisk assaults were made by the Germans in the Armentières area, one upon the Fourth Division of the Third Corps and the other upon the Seaforth Highlanders, who were brigaded with the Indians. In each case the first German rush carried some trenches, and in each the swift return of the British regained them. There were moderate losses upon both sides. On the same date the 13th Infantry Brigade lost the services of Colonel Martyn of the 1st West Kents, who was seriously wounded the very day after he had been appointed to a brigade.

This attack upon November 11 represents the absolute high-water mark of the German efforts in this battle, and the ebb was a rapid one. Upon November 12 and the remainder of the week, halfhearted attempts were made upon the British front, which were repulsed without difficulty. To the north of the line, where the French had held their positions with much the same fluctuations which had been experienced by their Allies, the German assault was more violent and met with occasional success, though it was finally repelled with very great loss. The 14th was to the French what the 11th had been to the British – the culmination of violence and the prelude of rest. The weather throughout this period was cold and tempestuous, which much increased the strain upon the weary troops. Along the whole line from Ypres to Bethune there were desultory shellings with an occasional dash by one side or the other, which usually ended in the capture of a trench and its recapture by the supports in the rear. It was in one of these sporadic German attacks in the Klein Zillebeke section that the 2nd King's Royal Rifles held their trench against heavy odds, and their machine-gun officer, Lieutenant Dimmer, thrice wounded and still fighting, won the coveted Cross by his valour. Each gallant advance and capture of the Germans was countered by an equally gallant counterattack and recapture by the British. The long line sagged and swayed, but never bent or broke. The era of battles had passed, but for thirty miles the skirmishes were incessant. So mixed and incessant had been the fighting that it was a very difficult task during these days to tidy up the line and get each scattered group of men back to its own platoon, company, and battalion.

On Tuesday, November 17, the fighting suddenly assumed a more important character. The attack was again in the Ypres section and fell chiefly upon the battalions of the Second Corps, if so dignified a name as " battalion " can be given to bodies of men which consisted very often of less than a normal company, commanded, perhaps, by two junior officers. The 4th Brigade of Guards was also heavily engaged this day, and so were the cavalry of the Third Division. The general locale of the action was the same as that which had been so often fought over before, the Second Corps being to the south of the Ypres-Menin road, with Lord Cavan's Guardsmen upon their right and the cavalry upon the right of the Guards. After a severe shelling there was a serious infantry advance, about one o'clock, which took some trenches, but was finally driven back and chased for a quarter of a mile. McCracken's 7th Brigade bore a chief part in this fighting, and the 1st Wiltshires particularly distinguished themselves by a fine charge led by Captain Cary-Barnard. The 2nd Grenadiers did great work during the day.

An even heavier advance was made in the afternoon to the south of that which was broken in the morning. This involved an oblique advance across the British front, which was stopped and destroyed before it reached the trenches by the deadly fire of rifles and machine-guns. Over a thousand dead were left as a proof of the energy of the attack and the solidity of the resistance. Farther to the south a similar attack was beaten back by the cavalry after a preliminary shelling in which the 3rd Dragoon Guards suffered severely. This attack was repelled by the Third Cavalry Division, to which the Leicestershire and North Somerset Yeomanry were now attached. The latter did fine service in this action. Altogether, November 17 was a good day for the British arms and a most expensive one for the Germans.

We have now reached the end of the Battle of Ypres, which attained its maximum fury, so far as the British line was concerned, from October 29 to November 11. This great contest raged from the sand dunes of the north, where the Belgians fought so well, through the French Marine Brigade at Dixmude, and the Ninth French Corps, to General Haig's Corps, which was buttressed on the right towards the latter part of the battle by the Sixteenth French Corps. Farther south yet another French corps supported and eventually took the place of the British cavalry opposite the lost villages of Wytschaete and Messines. From there ran the unbroken lines of the imperturbable Third Corps, which ended to the south in the trenches originally held by the Second British Corps, and later by the Indians. Across the La Bassée Canal the French once again took up the defence.

We have now arrived at what may be called the great winter lull, when the continuation of active operations was made impossible by the weather conditions, which were of the most atrocious description. It was the season which in a more classic age of warfare was spent in comfortable winter quarters. There was no such surcease of hardship for the contending lines, who were left in their trenches face to face, often not more than fifty yards apart, and each always keenly alert for any devilry upon the part of the other. The ashes of war were always redly smouldering, and sometimes, as will be seen, burst up into sudden furious flame. It was a period of rainstorms and of frost-bites, of trench mortars and of grenades, of weary, muddy, goat-skinned men shivering in narrow trenches, and of depleted brigades resting and recruiting in the rearward towns. Such was the position at the Front. But hundreds of miles to the westward the real future of the war was being fought out in the rifle factories of Birmingham, the great gun works of Woolwich, Coventry, Newcastle, and Sheffield, the cloth looms of Yorkshire, and the boot centres of Northampton. In these and many other places oversea the tools for victory were forged night and day through one of the blackest and most strenuous winters that Britain has ever known. And always on green and waste and common, from Cromarty to Brighton, wherever soldiers could find billets or a village of log huts could be put together, the soldier citizens who were to take up the burden of the war, the men of the Territorials and the men of the new armies, endured every hardship and discomfort without a murmur, whilst they prepared themselves for that great and glorious task which the future would bring. Even those who were too old or too young for service formed themselves into volunteer bands, who armed and clothed themselves at their own expense. This movement, which sprang first from the small Sussex village of Crowborough, was co-ordinated and controlled by a central body of which Lord Desborough was the head. In spite of discouragement, or at the best cold neutrality from Government, it increased and prospered until no fewer than a quarter of a million of men were mustered and ready entirely at their own expense and by private enterprise – one of the most remarkable phenomena of the war.

The Winter Lull of 1914

THE winter lull may be said to have extended from the great combats at Ypres of the middle of November to the opening of the spring campaign in March 1915; but we will only follow it here up to the end of the year. It was a period of alternate rest and discomfort for the troops with an ever-present salt of danger. For days they found themselves billeted with some approach to comfort in the farmhouses and villages of Flanders, but such brief intervals of peace were broken by the routine of the trenches, when, in mud or water with a clay cutting before their faces and another at their backs, they waited through the long hours, listening to the crack of the sniper's rifle, or the crash of the bursting shell, with an indifference which bordered upon thankfulness for anything that would break the drab monotony of their task. It was a scene of warfare which was new to military experience. The vast plain of battle lay in front of the observer as a flat and lonely wilderness, dotted with ruined houses from which no homely wreath of smoke rose into the wintry air. Here and there was an untidy litter of wire; here and there also a clump of bleak and tattered woodland; but nowhere was there any sign of man. And yet from the elevation of an aeroplane it might be seen that the population of a large city was lurking upon that motionless waste. Everywhere the airman would have distinguished the thin brown slits of the advance trenches, the broader ditches of the supports and the long zigzags of the communications, and he would have detected that they were stuffed with men – grey men and khaki, in every weird garment that ingenuity could suggest for dryness and for warmth – all cowering within their shelters with the ever-present double design of screening themselves and of attacking their enemy. As the German pressure became less, and as more regiments of the Territorials began to arrive, taking some of the work from their comrades of the Regulars, it was possible to mitigate something of the discomforts of warfare, to ensure that no regiments should be left for too long a period in the trenches, and even to arrange for week-end visits to England for a certain number of officers and men. The streets of London got a glimpse of rugged, war-hardened faces, and of uniforms caked with the brown mud of Flanders, or supplemented by strange Robinson Crusoe goat-skins from the trenches, which brought home to the least imaginative the nature and the nearness of the struggle.

To take events in their order: beyond numerous gallant affairs of outposts, there was no incident of importance until the evening of November 23, when the Germans, who had seemed stunned for a week or so, showed signs of returning animation. On this day, some eight hundred yards of trench held by Indian troops in the neighbourhood of Armentières were made untenable by the German artillery, especially by the *Minenwerfe* – small mortars which threw enormous bombs by an ingenious arrangement whereby the actual shell never entered the bore but was on the end of a rod outside the muzzle. Some of these terrible missiles, which came through the air as slowly as a punted football, were 200 lbs. in weight and shattering in their effects. There was an advance of the 112th Regiment of the Fourteenth German Corps, and the empty trenches were strongly occupied by them – so strongly that the first attempt to retake them was unsuccessful in the face of the rifle and machine-gun fire of the defenders. A second more powerful counter-attack was organised by General Anderson of the Meerut Division, and this time the Germans were swept out of their position and the line re-established. The fighting lasted all night, and the Ghurkas with their formidable knives proved to be invaluable for such close work, while a party of Engineers with hand-bombs did great execution – a strange combination of the Asiatic with the most primitive of weapons and the scientific European with the most recent. It was a substantial victory as such affairs go, for the British were left with a hundred prisoners, including three officers, three machine-guns, and two mortars.

The first week of December was rendered memorable by a visit of the King to the Army. King George reviewed a great number of his devoted soldiers, who showed by their fervent enthusiasm that one need not be an autocratic Warlord in order to command the fierce loyalty of the legions. After this pleasant interlude there followed a succession of those smaller exploits which seem so slight in any chronicle, and yet collectively do so much to sustain the spirit of the Army. Now this dashing officer, now that, attempted some deed upon the German line, and never failed to find men to follow him to death. On November 24 it was Lieutenant Impey, with a handful of 2nd Lincolns; on November 25, Lieutenants Ford and Morris with a few Welsh Fusiliers and sappers; on November 26, Sir Edward Hulse with some Scots Guards; on the same day. Lieutenant Durham with men of the 2nd Rifle Brigade – in each case trenches were temporarily won, the enemy was damaged, and a spirit of adventure encouraged in the trenches. Sometimes such a venture ended in the death of the leader, as in the case of Captain the Honourable H. L. Bruce of the Royal Scots. Such men died as the old knights did who rode out betwixt the lines of marshalled armies, loved by their friends and admired by their foes.

King George visits the troops.

December 9 was the date of two small actions. In the first the 1st Lincolns of the 9th Brigade, which had been commanded by Douglas Smith since the wounding of General Shaw, made an attack upon the wood at Wytschaete which is called Le Petit Bois. The advance was not successful, the three officers who led it being all wounded, and forty-four men being hit. The attempt was renewed upon a larger scale five days later. The other action was an attack by the enemy upon some of the trenches of the Third Corps. This Corps, though it had not come in for the more dramatic scenes of the campaign, had done splendid and essential work in covering a line of fourteen miles or so against incessant attacks of the Germans, who never were able to gain any solid advantage. On this occasion the impact fell upon Gordon's 19th Brigade, especially upon the 2nd Argyll and Sutherland Highlanders and the 1st Middlesex. It was driven back with heavy loss.

On December 14 the second and more sustained effort was made to get possession of the Petit Bois at Wytschaete, which had been attacked by the Lincolns upon the 9th. D'Urbal's Eighth French Army was co-operating upon the left. The British attack was conducted by Haldane's Third Division, and the actual advance was carried out, after a considerable artillery preparation from the batteries of two Corps, by Bowes' 8th Brigade, with the 2nd Royal Scots and the 1st Gordons in the lead. At 7:45 the guns were turned upon the big wood beyond Petit Bois, through which the supports might be advancing, and at the same hour the two regiments named swarmed forward, the Lowlanders on the left and the Highlanders on the right. The Royal Scots, under Major Duncan, carried Petit Bois with a rush, taking fifty prisoners and two machine-guns, while the Germans fled out at the other end of the wood. The Scots at once entrenched themselves and got their own machine guns into position. The Gordons, under Major Baird, advanced with splendid dash and gained some ground, but found the position such that they could not entrench upon it, so they were forced to fall back eventually to their original position. Both they and the 4th Middlesex, who supported them, lost considerably in the affair. The total casualties in the Petit Bois action came to over four hundred, with seventeen officers, figures which were considerably swollen by the losses of the Suffolks and Irish Rifles, who continued to hold the captured position in the face of continued bombing. The French in the north had no particular success and lost 600 men. The importance of such operations is not to be measured, however, by the amount of ground won, but by the necessity of beating up the enemies' quarters, keeping them pinned to their positions, and preventing them from feeling that they could at their own sweet wills detach any reinforcements they chose to thicken their line upon the Eastern frontier, where our Russian Allies were so insistently pressing.

On the morning of December 19 an attack was made upon the German lines in the Festubert region by Willcocks' Indian Corps, the Meerut Division, under General Anderson, attacking upon the left, and the Lahore, under General Watkis, upon the right. The object of the movement was to co-operate with the French in an advance which they had planned. The Meerut attack was successful at first, but was driven back by a counter-attack, and some hundreds of Indian infantry were killed, wounded, or taken. In the case of the Lahore attack the storming party consisted of the 1st Highland Light Infantry and the 4th Ghurkas. Both of these units belong to the Sirhind Brigade, but they were joined in the enterprise by the 59th Scinde Rifles of the Jullundur Brigade. These latter troops had a long night march before reaching the scene of the operations, when they found themselves upon the right of the attack and within two hundred and fifty yards of the German trenches. Judging the operations from the standard reached at a later date, the whole arrangement seems to have been extraordinarily primitive. The artillery preparation for a frontal attack upon a strong German line of trenches lasted exactly four minutes, being rather a call to arms than a bombardment. The troops rushed most gallantly forward into the dark of a cold wet winter morning, with no guide save the rippling flashes of the rifles and machine-guns in front of them. Many were so sore-footed and weary that they could not break into the double. Some of the Indians were overtaken from behind by a line of British supports, which caused considerable confusion. An officer of Indians has left it on record that twice running he had a revolver clapped to his head by a British officer. All of the battalions advanced with a frontage of two companies in columns of platoons. Both the Ghurkas and Highlanders reached the trench in the face of a murderous fire. The left of the 59th, consisting of Punjabi Mahomedans, also reached the trench. The right, who were Sikhs, made an equally gallant advance, but were knee-deep in a wet beetroot field and under terrific machine-gun fire. Their gallant leader, Captain Scale, was struck down, as was every Indian officer, but a handful of the survivors, under a Sikh Jemadar, got into a German sap, which they held for twenty-four hours, taking a number of prisoners.

Day had dawned, and though the British and Indians were in the enemy trenches, it was absolutely impossible to send them up reinforcements across the bullet-swept plain. The 59th discovered a sap running from their left to the German line, and along this they pushed. They could not get through, however, to where their comrades were being terribly bombed on either flank by the counter-attack. It was an heroic resistance. Colonel Ronaldson, who led the party, held on all day, but was very lucky in being able to withdraw most of the survivors after nightfall. Of the hundred Punjabis who held one flank, only three returned, while thirteen wounded were reported later from Germany. The others all refused to surrender, declaring that those were the last orders of their British officers, and so they met their honoured end. It had been a long and weary day with a barren ending, for all that had been won was abandoned. The losses were over a thousand, and were especially heavy in the case of officers.

The Germans, elated by the failure of the attack, were in the mood for a return visit. In the early dawn of the next day, December 20, they began a heavy bombardment of the Indian trenches, followed by an infantry attack extending over a line of six miles from south of the Bethune Canal to Festubert in the north. The attack began by the explosion of a succession of mines which inflicted very heavy losses upon the survivors of the Ghurkas and Highland Light Infantry. The weight of the attack at the village of Givenchy fell upon the exhausted Sirhind Heavy Brigade, who were driven back, and the greater part of Givenchy was occupied by the enemy. General Brunker fell back with his Brigade, but his line was stiffened by the arrival of the 47th Sikhs of the 8th Jullundur Brigade, who were in divisional reserve. These troops prevented any further advance of the Germans, while preparations were made for an effective counter-stroke.

Little help could be given from the north, where the line was already engaged, but to the south there were considerable bodies of troops available. The situation was serious, and a great effort was called for, since it was impossible to abandon into the hands of the enemy a village which was an essential bastion upon the line of defence. The German attack had flooded down south of Givenchy to the Bethune Canal, and a subsidiary attack had come along the south of the Canal with the object of holding the troops in their places and preventing the reinforcement of the defenders of Givenchy. But these advances south of the village made no progress, being held up by the 9th Bhopals and Wilde's 57th Rifles of the 7th Ferozepore Brigade between Givenchy and the canal, while the 1st Connaught Rangers of the same brigade stopped it on the southern side of the canal. Matters were for a moment in equilibrium. To the south of the canal energetic measures were taken to get together a force which could come across it by the Pont Fixe or road bridge, and reestablish matters in the north.

The struggle had broken out close to the point of junction between the British forces and those of General Foch of the Tenth French Army, so that our Allies were able to co-operate with us in the counter-attack. It was directed by General Carnegy, and the assault was made by the 1st Manchesters, the 4th Suffolk Territorials, and some French territorials. The Manchesters, under the leadership of Colonel Strickland, made a most notable attack, aided by two companies of the Suffolks, the other companies remaining in reserve on the north bank of the canal. So critical was the position that the 3rd Indian Sappers and Miners were set the dangerous task, under very heavy shell-fire, of mining the bridge over the canal. The situation was saved, however, by Colonel Strickland's fine advance. His infantry, with very inadequate artillery support, pushed its way into Givenchy and cleared the village from end to end. Three hundred of the Manchesters fell in this deed of arms. Not only did they win the village, but they also regained some of the lost trenches to the north-east of Givenchy. This was the real turning-point of the action. There was at the time only the one very wet, very weary, and rather cut-up Jullundur Brigade between the Germans and Bethune – with all that Bethune stood for strategically. To the east the 9th Bhopals and 57th Rifles still held on to their position. It was only to the north that the enemy retained his lodgment.

But the fight to the north had been a bitter one all day, and had gone none too well for the British forces. The Indians were fighting at an enormous disadvantage. As well turn a tiger loose upon an ice-floe and expect that he will show all his wonted fierceness and activity. There are inexorable axioms of Nature which no human valour nor constancy can change. The bravest of the brave, our Indian troops were none the less the children of the sun, dependent upon warmth for their vitality and numbed by the cold wet life of the trenches. That they still in the main maintained a brave, uncomplaining, soldierly demeanour, and that they made head against the fierce German assaults, is a wonderful proof of their adaptability.

About ten o'clock on the morning of the 20th the German attack, driving back the Sirhind Brigade from Givenchy, who were the left advanced flank of the Lahore Division, came with a rush against the Dehra-Dun Brigade, who were the extreme right of the Meerut Division. This Brigade had the 1st Seaforth Highlanders upon its flank, with the 2nd Ghurkas upon its left. The Ghurkas were forced to retire, and the almost simultaneous retirement of the defenders of Givenchy left the Highlanders in a desperate position with both flanks in the air. Fortunately the next Brigade of the Meerut Division, the Garhwal Brigade, stood fast and kept in touch with the 6th Jats, who formed the left of the Dehra Dun Brigade, and so prevented the pressure upon that side from becoming intolerable. The 9th Ghurkas came up to support the 2nd Ghurkas, who had not

Indian soldiers in France.

gone far from their abandoned trenches, and the 58th Indian Rifles also came to the front. These battalions upon the left rear of the Highlanders gave them some support. None the less the position of the battalion was dangerous and its losses heavy, but it faced the Germans with splendid firmness, and nothing could budge it. Machine-guns are stronger than flesh and blood, but the human spirit can be stronger than either. You might kill the Highlanders, but you could not shift them. The 2nd Black Watch, who had been in reserve, established touch towards nightfall with the right of the Seaforths, and also with the left of the Sirhind Brigade, so that a continuous line was assured.

In the meantime a small force had assembled under General MacBean with the intention of making a counter-attack and recovering the ground which had been lost on the north side of Givenchy, With the 8th Ghurkas and the 47th Sikhs, together with the 7th British Dragoon Guards, an attack was made in the early hours of the 21st. Colonel Lempriere of the

Dragoon Guards was killed, and the attack failed. It was renewed in the early hours of the morning, but it again failed to dislodge the Germans from the captured trenches.

December 21 dawned upon a situation which was not particularly rosy from a British point of view. It is true that Givenchy had been recovered, but a considerable stretch of trenches were still in the hands of the Germans, their artillery was exceedingly masterful, and the British line was weakened by heavy losses and indented in several places. The one bright spot was the advance of the First Division of Haig's Corps, who had come up in the night-time. The three brigades of this Division were at once thrown into the fight, the first being sent to Givenchy, the second given as a support to the Meerut Division, and the third directed upon the trenches which had been evacuated the day before by the Sirhind Brigade. All of these brigades won their way forward, and by the morning of the 22nd much of the ground which had been taken by the Germans was reoccupied by the British. The 1st Brigade, led by the Cameron Highlanders, had made good all the ground between Givenchy and the canal. Meanwhile the 3rd Brigade had re-established the Festubert position, where the 2nd Welsh and 1st South Wales Borderers had won their way into the lost trenches of the Ghurkas. This was not done without very stark fighting, in which of all the regiments engaged none suffered so heavily as the 2nd Munsters (now attached to the 3rd Brigade). This regiment, only just built up again after its practical extermination at Étreux in August, made a grand advance and fought without cessation for nearly forty-eight hours. Their losses were dreadful, including their gallant Colonel Bent, both Majors Day and Thomson, five other officers, and several hundreds of the rank and file. So far forward did they get that it was with great difficulty that the survivors, through the exertions of Major Ryan, were got back into a place of safety. It was the second of three occasions upon which this gallant Celtic battalion gave itself for King and Country. Let this soften the asperity of politics if unhappily we must come back to them after the war.

Meanwhile the lines upon the flank of the Seaforths which had been lost by the Dehra-Dun Brigade were carried by the 2nd Brigade (Westmacott), the 1st North Lancashire and 1st Northamptons leading the attack with the 2nd Rifles in support. Though driven back by a violent counter-attack in which both leading regiments, and especially the Lancashire men, lost heavily, the Brigade came again, and ended by making good the gap in the line. Thus the situation on the morning of the 22nd looked very much better than upon the day before. On this morning, as so many of the 1st Corps were in the advanced line, Sir Douglas Haig took over the command from Sir James Willcocks. The line had been to some extent re-established and the firing died away, but there were some trenches which were not retaken till a later date.

Such was the scrambling and unsatisfactory fight of Givenchy, a violent interlude in the drab records of trench warfare. It began with a considerable inroad of Germans into our territory and heavy losses of our Indian Contingent. It ended by a general return of the Germans to their former lines, and the resumption by the veteran troops of the First Division of the main positions which we had lost. Neither side had gained any ground of material value, but the balance of profit in captures was upon the side of the Germans, who may fairly claim that the action was a minor success for their arms, since they assert that they captured some hundreds of prisoners and several machine-guns. The Anglo-Indian Corps had 2600 casualties, and the First Corps 1400, or 4000 in all. The Indian troops were now withdrawn for a rest, which they had well earned by their long and difficult service in the trenches. To stand day after day up to his knees in ice-cold water is no light ordeal for a European, but it is difficult to imagine all that it must have been to a Southern Asiatic. The First Corps took over the La Bassée lines.

About the same date as the Battle of Givenchy there was some fighting farther north at Rouge Banc, where the Fourth Corps was engaged and some German trenches were taken. The chief losses in this affair fell upon those war-worn units, the 2nd Scots Guards and 2nd Borderers of the 20th Brigade. Henceforward peace reigned along the lines for several weeks

– indeed Christmas brought about something like fraternisation between British and Germans, who found a sudden and extraordinary link in that ancient tree worship, long anterior to Christianity, which Saxon tribes had practised in the depths of Germanic forests and still commemorated by their candle-lit firs. For a single day the opposing forces mingled in friendly conversation and even in games. It was an amazing spectacle, and must arouse bitter thoughts concerning those high-born conspirators against the peace of the world, who in their mad ambition had hounded such men on to take each other by the throat rather than by the hand. For a day there was comradeship. But the case had been referred to the God of Battles, and the doom had not yet been spoken. It must go to the end. On the morning of the 26th dark figures vanished reluctantly into the earth, and the rifles cracked once more. It remains one human episode amid all the atrocities which have stained the memory of the war.

So ended 1914, the year of resistance. During it the Western Allies had been grievously oppressed by their well-prepared enemy. They had been overweighted by numbers and even more so by munitions. For a space it had seemed as if the odds were too much for them. Then with a splendid

The haunting landscape of no-man's land.

rally they had pushed the enemy back. But his reserves had come up and had proved to be as superior as his first line had been. But even so he had reached his limit. He could get no further. The danger hour was past. There was now coming the long, anxious year of equilibrium, the narrative of which will be given in the succeeding volume of 1915. Finally will come the year of restoration which will at least begin, though it will not finish, the victory of the champions of freedom.